YOUR
HEALTHCARE
JOB HUNT

YOUR

HEALTHCARE Q

JOB HUNT

How Your Digital Presence Can 👍 Make or Break 👎 Your Career

Donna Malvey | Jessica Sapp

ACHE Management Series

Library of Congress Cataloging-in-Publication Data
Names: Malvey, Donna M., author. | Sapp, Jessica, author. | American College of Healthcare Executives, issuing body.
Title: Your healthcare job hunt : how your digital presence can make or break your career / Donna Malvey, Jessica Sapp.
Other titles: Management series (Ann Arbor, Mich.)
Description: Chicago, IL : Health Administration Press, [2020] | Series: HAP/ACHE management series | Includes bibliographical references and index. | Summary: "This book explains how the job seeker's digital presence affects the success of a healthcare job hunt. It covers information, tools, and internet resources—including social media—that can help job candidates stand out and maximize their career advancement opportunities"— Provided by publisher.
Identifiers: LCCN 2020007643 (print) | LCCN 2020007644 (ebook) | ISBN 9781640551756 (paperback : alk. paper) | ISBN 9781640551763 (ebook) | ISBN 9781640551770 (epub) | ISBN 9781640551787 (mobi)
Subjects: MESH: Health Personnel | Internet | Online Social Networking | Employment | Career Choice
Classification: LCC R727 (print) | LCC R727 (ebook) | NLM W 21 | DDC 610.73/ 7069—dc23
LC record available at https://lccn.loc.gov/2020007643
LC ebook record available at https://lccn.loc.gov/2020007644

The paper used in this publication meets the minimum requirements of American National Standard for Information Sciences—Permanence of Paper for Printed Library Materials, ANSI Z39.48-1984. ♾ ™

Acquisitions editor: Janet Davis; Project editor: Andrew Baumann; Cover designer: Brad Norr; Layout: Integra

Found an error or a typo? We want to know! Please e-mail it to hapbooks@ache.org, mentioning the book's title and putting "Book Error" in the subject line.

For photocopying and copyright information, please contact Copyright Clearance Center at www.copyright.com or at (978) 750-8400.

Health Administration Press
A division of the Foundation of the American
   College of Healthcare Executives
300 S. Riverside Plaza, Suite 1900
Chicago, IL 60606-6698
(312) 424-2800

Contents

Introduction | vii

Chapter 1: Google You | 1

Chapter 2: Self-Discovery | 7

Chapter 3: Digital Self-Perception | 17

Chapter 4: Digital Self-Branding | 31

Chapter 5: Self-Determined Career | 51

Chapter 6: Self-Learning | 63

Chapter 7: Job Prep | 75

Chapter 8: Interviews | 91

Chapter 9: Digital Networking | 107

Chapter 10: Self-Evaluation | 115

Chapter 11: Social Media Tips | 121

Chapter 12: Going Off-Screen | 131

Index | 145

About the Authors | 155

Introduction

WHEN YOU WANT to know something, what do you do? You grab your smartphone, say "Okay Google" (or "Hey Siri" if you have an iPhone), and then ask your voice assistant what you want to know. You can find nearby restaurants, look for specific businesses, read product reviews, and get trivia answers or the latest entertainment gossip. With the internet, you can find so much in mere seconds.

But what if you're thinking about applying for a job and you can't find any information online about the prospective employer? Do you begin to question the credibility of the organization? Do you wonder if the job listing is a scam? Everything is online, so why can't you find anything about the company on the internet?

Now let's reverse the situation. What if an employer can't find *you* online? What message does this send to a hiring manager or organization? Did you know that more than half of employers (57 percent) won't hire you if you don't have an online presence, and most employers (70 percent) will use social media to screen your application (Connley 2017)? So, just as important as having an online presence is ensuring that your online persona accurately reflects how you want to be seen as a professional.

We use online information to make informed decisions and to make our daily tasks easier. We can also use the internet to learn about potential employers or to apply for job openings. In today's job market, more and more employers are using online tools and social media to collect job applications. Many companies are recruiting job candidates through sites such as LinkedIn and posting career opportunities on job boards such as Indeed. With the increasing use of technology and digital interactions, having a professional online presence is essential to career advancement and networking.

Networking has evolved and, with the digital environment, has entered a new era. Digital tools such as social media and e-mail have made more people accessible to you for networking and mentoring because they are no longer restricted by geographic location. According to a survey undertaken by Lou Adler, CEO of Performance-based Hiring Learning Systems and designated LinkedIn influencer, 85 percent of respondents identified networking as their primary means for finding a job (Adler 2016). Although face-to-face (offline) networking is also necessary to maximize your opportunities, using the digital environment for virtual networking is critical.

If you are ready to be your best online self and learn how to pair your online presence with your offline career aspirations, then start with this book, *Your Healthcare Job Hunt: How Your Digital Presence Can Make or Break Your Career.*

REFERENCES

Adler, L. 2016. "New Survey Reveals 85% of All Jobs Are Filled via Networking." LinkedIn. Published February 29. www.linkedin.com/pulse/new-survey-reveals-85-all-jobs-filled-via-networking-lou-adler/.

Connley, C. 2017. "More Than Half of Employers Won't Hire Someone They Can't Find Online." CNBC. Published August 18. www.cnbc.com/2017/08/18/more-than-half-of-employers-wont-hire-someone-they-cant-find-online.html.

CHAPTER 1

Google You

YOU HAVE LIKELY Googled your favorite celebrity or a potential romantic partner, but have you ever Googled yourself? Your online persona can say a lot about you, but is it telling the right story? We are living in a digital age, one in which more and more people are sharing information with others through social media and the internet. The online environment makes it easy for people to find details about you through what is known as your "digital footprint." You need to understand what information is available online about you, because prospective employers will search for it.

Can you answer yes to any of the following questions?

- Do you have a Facebook, Twitter, Instagram, or other social networking account?
- Do you post photos or selfies on social media?
- Have you ever been tagged in a photo on social media?
- Are there photos anywhere online showing you at a party or drinking alcohol?
- Have you been tagged in a photo taken at a bachelor or bachelorette party?
- Are there photos online in which you are smoking?

- Are there any online photos of you receiving an award?
- Have you posted graduation photos on social media?
- Have you made any social media posts or comments that could be interpreted negatively?
- Have you "liked" someone else's post that others might consider offensive?

If you answered yes to any of these items, you must understand that prospective employers and professional colleagues have access to this information. Is the image of you that they'll find online the one you want to share with them?

CHAPTER KEYWORDS

- Digital (or online) profile
- Digital (or internet) footprint
- Internet search

WEB BROWSERS AND SEARCH ENGINES

We often say "Google it" when we talk about searching for something on the internet, but multiple web browsers and search engines are, in fact, available. Google Chrome, Microsoft Edge, Internet Explorer, Firefox, and Safari are examples of web browsers. Each uses different algorithms and techniques to pull information from the Web. You use a browser to access a search engine, such as Google, Bing, or Yahoo! To maximize your search results, you should conduct searches using different web browsers and search engines.

SEARCHING YOURSELF BY NAME AND KEYWORDS

There are various ways to search for yourself online. The most common and straightforward is by keywords, since this is how search engines typically retrieve information. Start with your first and last name as search words. If you have a common name, you may not immediately get a lot of relevant results unless you have a popular online activity, such as a viral YouTube video or Twitter post. If you have had multiple names (e.g., because of marriage or other legal name changes), you should check all of them. If you use a nickname, search it, too.

What comes up when you search your name?

- Do you see your graduation pictures?
- Do you see your LinkedIn profile page?
- Do you see information about your home address?
- Did you find an online blog article you wrote?
- Did you find a social media post about a crazy party you attended?
- Did you find any photos showing drinking or hazing with you in them?

After you have searched your first and last name, try searching your name with different affiliated organizations or activities, such as your college, hobbies, sports (ones you play or events you attend), extracurricular activities, and jobs (exhibit 1.1). For example, to search your first and last name with your college, type "John Smith UF" or "John Smith University of Florida." Multiple searches will give you more results. Search your name with each organization and activity.

EXHIBIT 1.1: Sample Searches

Search term—name	Search term—keyword	Example
First and last name	College	John Smith UCLA
First and last name	Organization	Mitchell Williams American College of Healthcare Executives
First and last name	Employer	Jennifer Watson Blue Cross Blue Shield
First and last name	Volunteer organization	Julio Rodriguez American Cancer Society
First and last name	Job title	Lisa Jones administrative assistant
First and last name	Extracurricular activity	Helen Miller debate competition
First and last name	Student organization	Timothy Brown Health Services Administration Student Association
First and last name	Sport	Jaylen Johnson football
First and last name	Hobby	Tiana Wilson singing
First and last name	City	Jacqueline Torres Houston
First and last name	Arrest	James Davis arrest
First and last name	Mug shot	Marie Nguyen mug shot

Note: The names used in these examples are fictitious and not those of real people.

Anyone with basic information about you can conduct such searches, so it's good to understand what they will find. Remember that college party you attended—can it be found online by searching your name and alma mater? The schools you attended are listed on your resume and LinkedIn profile, so potential

employers and other professionals will have access to this
information.

Repeat these searches using
multiple web browsers and
search engines. Log your results
so that you can address any negative ones. (We'll show you how
to fix these in chapter 4, "Digital
Self-Branding.")

Searching your name
online may also help
prevent identify theft. If
someone else is falsely
using your name, you
may find it online.

CHECK IMAGE RESULTS, TOO

When you conduct an online search, the search engine will include
images and videos among the results. In most web browsers, you
have to click on an "Images" tab to retrieve the image search results.
Viewing these images is important because you may find some that
you didn't know were posted online. Your friends and family may
have posted photos of you on social media or on internet sites that
can be searched using your name, especially if they tagged you in
the photos.

The post you tag the person in may also be added to that
person's timeline. For example, you can tag a photo to show
who's in the photo or post a status update and say who you're
with. If you tag a friend in your status update, anyone who
sees that update can click on your friend's name and go to
their profile.

—Facebook (2019)

Action Items

1. Search your name on the internet, with and without keywords.
2. Log the results for each search.
3. Repeat your searches using different web browsers and search engines.
4. Identify any negative or unflattering items.

CHAPTER SUMMARY

Your digital profile should reflect who you are professionally. Understanding what exists online about you is the first step toward improving your online persona—that is, how others perceive you online. As you read this book, you will learn about your digital footprint and the importance of developing your online profile.

RESOURCE

Moz. "The Beginner's Guide to SEO." https://moz.com/beginners-guide-to-seo.

REFERENCE

Facebook. 2019. "What Is Tagging and How Does It Work?" Accessed May 1. www.facebook.com/help/124970597582337/.

CHAPTER 2

Self-Discovery

THE TERM "SELF-DISCOVERY" has various meanings. It can mean learning more about your character, attributes, and values, but it can also extend to understanding your professional strengths and abilities. Knowing your strengths, weaknesses, likes, dislikes, and abilities can offer valuable insights for your healthcare career. What you learn in self-discovery can help align your digital path with your healthcare career goals.

CHAPTER KEYWORDS

- Career goals
- Self-assessments
- Self-discovery

CAREER GOALS

Goals are the stepping-stones of your career path. There are short-term goals and long-term goals, and understanding how to plan your goals will help you self-determine your career (discussed further in chapter 5).

Students often talk about becoming a hospital CEO or other top-level executive soon after graduating with a bachelor's degree, despite having no experience. Can it happen? Possibly. But like winning the lotto, is it likely? No. In fact, unrealistic goals can distract you from advancing on your career path.

You need to set realistic career goals to get where you want to be within the next few years. If you aspire to be a hospital CEO in your lifetime, you can begin your journey by developing goals that will help you gain the knowledge, skills, and experience that such a senior healthcare executive position requires. To begin, you need to evaluate your current knowledge, skills, and experience so that you can compare them with what will be required.

Your journey is likelier to succeed if you set SMART goals—that is, goals that are specific, measurable, achievable, relevant, and time-bound (Doran 1981). You may recall this from a college class or other instructional venue, such as a conference. Establish where you want your career to be in five years, and then develop a plan using one-year increments and create your goals accordingly. What is achievable in Year 1? Year 2? Year 3? And so on.

Finally, always remember why you decided to go into healthcare. Do you want to help people? Did a nurse make an impact on you while a loved one was receiving care in a hospital? Did a medical doctor save your life? Did someone else in healthcare inspire you? Identifying your motivations will keep you focused and driven to achieve your goals.

Success is a journey. We don't stop achieving or growing when we reach our goals. We keep learning and climbing towards our next dream.

—Sapp (2019)

SELF-ASSESSMENT TOOLS

You can evaluate your current knowledge, skills, and experience by taking one or more self-assessments. Numerous assessments are used in various industries, and a few are very well known. Among those commonly used are personality tests, emotional intelligence (EI) tests, and healthcare competency assessments.

- **Myers-Briggs Type Indicator (MBTI):** The MBTI assessment determines your personality type according to your psychological preferences. There are 16 unique types, based on four preference scales: (1) extraversion versus introversion, (2) sensing versus intuition, (3) thinking versus feeling, and (4) judging versus perceiving.

- **Fundamental Interpersonal Relations Orientation– Behavior (FIRO-B):** The FIRO-B instrument identifies your interpersonal needs for inclusion, control, and affection and assesses how they influence your communication style and behavior. A related assessment, FIRO Business, addresses the specific requirements of organizations by identifying your interpersonal needs for involvement, influence, and connection.

- **Emotional intelligence:** EI is the capacity to be aware of, control, and express your own emotions and to understand the emotions of others so that you can handle interpersonal relationships empathetically and appropriately. Although your EI has been identified as a major contributor to your success as a leader, it is influential at all stages of your career. EI has five components: self-awareness, self-regulation, motivation, empathy, and social skills.

- **DISC:** The DISC assessment tool measures how you prefer to interact with others according to four behavioral styles: dominance, influence, steadiness, and conscientiousness. The Extended DISC Individual Assessment can be tailored to different industries, including healthcare.

- **Career Anchors:** Before you accept a job offer, you consider many factors, such as salary, purpose, career motivations, opportunity for promotion, job security, and work–life balance. How you rank these factors depends on your values and your career expectations. The Career Anchors self-assessment, developed by MIT professor emeritus Edgar Schein, ranks the importance to you of key elements, including autonomy, creativity, stability, and competence.

- **ACHE Healthcare Executive Competencies Assessment Tool:** The American College of Healthcare Executives (ACHE) developed this assessment tool for healthcare leaders, but it is valuable to healthcare administrators at all career levels. The tool is designed to help you identify strengths and areas in which you may need to develop skills for the healthcare environment. It assesses your expertise in five critical domains: (1) communication and relationship management, (2) leadership, (3) professionalism, (4) knowledge of the healthcare environment, and (5) business skills and knowledge. You can use this tool to create an action plan for self-learning (see chapter 6).

- **ACHE CareerEDGE:** ACHE's CareerEDGE is an interactive online tool that incorporates your self-assessment results, career goals, and career plan in a personalized dashboard. You can use career-planning tools, job site links, and other digital resources to plan your healthcare career path. This one-stop online solution is a complimentary benefit of ACHE membership.

OPEN-ACCESS ASSESSMENT TOOLS

Some of the top self-assessments must be purchased, but others are available to you free of charge. The following open-access tools are great resources to begin your self-discovery.

Personality Assessments

- **Jung Typology Test:** This assessment is based on Carl Jung's and Isabel Briggs Myers's personality type theory. It identifies your personality type from among the 16 personality types included in the Jung and Myers Briggs typology.
- **New Enneagram Test:** The Enneagram assessment identifies your personality type as one of nine: reformer, helper, motivator, romantic, thinker, skeptic, enthusiast, leader, and peacemaker.

Emotional Intelligence Assessments

- **MindTools' "How Emotionally Intelligent Are You?" test:** Some EI tests have hundreds of questions. This one uses only 15 questions to evaluate your EI.
- **Global Emotional Intelligence Test (GEIT):** The GEIT assessment uses 40 questions to score your skills in four areas: self-awareness, self-management, social awareness, and relationship management. It is derived from the Global Leadership Foundation's 158-question Global EI Capability Assessment.

Leadership Assessments

- **The Price Group's "True Leader" quiz:** This test uses 24 questions to assess your leadership style. Your collective score indicates the extent to which you lead versus manage.
- **Anthony J. Mayo's "Which Type of Leader Are You?" assessment:** According to Anthony J. Mayo and Nitin Nohria's book *In Their Time: The Greatest Business Leaders of the 20th Century*, brilliant leaders come in three types: the Entrepreneur, the Manager, and the Charismatic. This assessment evaluates which type of leader you are.

Learning Assessments

- **VARK questionnaire:** This assessment identifies your learning preferences according to four sensory modalities: visual, aural, reading/writing, and kinesthetic. Knowing your learning style can help you select the professional development opportunities that are best for you. Understanding your learning style is also beneficial when you are developing a self-learning plan to improve your skill set and advance your career.
- **Work values test:** This test is similar to the Career Anchors self-assessment in that it measures career values, but more values are included. The assessment measures autonomy, creativity, variety, structure, self-development, influence, work–life balance, financial reward, security, prestige, performance, working conditions, work relationships, and altruism.

Action Items

1. Take at least three self-assessments (and save your results).
2. Write down three to five career goals.

Now, applying what you learned about yourself through the self-assessments you took, determine if your strengths and abilities are reflected in your digital footprint. Do the offline and online versions of you exist in harmony? Using your internet search results from chapter 1, answer the following questions:

3. Who are you in the online environment? How do you perceive yourself based on your search results and self-assessments?
4. What is your online persona? How do others perceive you online?
5. Does your digital profile represent your career goals?

CHAPTER SUMMARY

Understanding your abilities and preferences allows you to enhance your strengths and improve your weaknesses. Self-discovery makes you aware of your knowledge, skills, and abilities, which will serve as the basis for your digital career plan.

RESOURCES

Smartsheet. "The Essential Guide to Writing S.M.A.R.T. Goals." www.smartsheet.com/blog/essential-guide-writing-smart-goals.

Self-Assessment Tools

ACHE CareerEDGE: www.ache.org/career-resource-center/ advance-your-career/career-edge.

ACHE Healthcare Executive Competencies Assessment Tool: www. ache.org/-/media/ache/career-resource-center/competencies_ booklet.pdf.

Career Anchors Self-Assessment: www.wiley.com/WileyCDA/ Section/id-822141.html (also available at www.ache.org/ career-resource-center/products-and-services/career-anchors-assessment).

DISC individual assessment: www.talentsmart.com/products/ idisc.php.

Emotional intelligence assessment: www.talentsmart.com/ products/emotional-intelligence-appraisal.php (also available at www.ache.org/career-resource-center/products-and-services/ emotional-intelligence-assessment).

Extended DISC individual assessment: www.ache.org/career-resource-center/products-and-services/extended-disc-assessment.

Myers-Briggs Type Indicator (MBTI) and Fundamental Interper-sonal Relations Orientation–Behavior (FIRO-B): www.mbtionline. com/TaketheMBTI and https://careerassessmentsite.com/ tests/firo-business-firo-b-tests/about-the-firo-b/ (also available together at www.ache.org/career-resource-center/products-and-services/leadership-assessment).

Open-Access Assessment Tools

Anthony J. Mayo's "Which Type of Leader Are You?" assessment: www.fastcompany.com/72686/which-type-leader-are-you.

Global Emotional Intelligence Test (GEIT): https://globalleadershipfoundation.com/geit/eitest.html.

Jung Typology Test: www.humanmetrics.com/cgi-win/jtypes2.asp.

Mind Tools' "How Emotionally Intelligent Are You?" test: www. mindtools.com/pages/article/ei-quiz.htm.

New Enneagram Test: www.9types.com/newtest/index.php.

Price Group's "True Leader" quiz: www.pricegroupleadership.com/ tl_quiz.shtml.

VARK questionnaire: http://vark-learn.com/the-vark-questionnaire/.

Work values test: www.123test.com/work-values-test/.

REFERENCES

Doran, G. 1981. "There's a S.M.A.R.T. Way to Write Management's Goals and Objectives." *Management Review*. Published November. https://community.mis.temple.edu/mis0855002fall2015/ files/2015/10/S.M.A.R.T-Way-Management-Review.pdf.

Sapp, J. 2019. "Home." Accessed March 30. www.drjessicasapp. com.

CHAPTER 3

Digital Self-Perception

TODAY, MOST JOB searches begin online. The recruiting and hiring processes require digital authenticity—that is, who you are online must match important documents such as your resume and assessments from previous employers. Consequently, understanding the role of digital self-perception is essential. This chapter will help you create a digital profile that is authentic and signals to employers the value you will contribute to their organization.

CHAPTER KEYWORDS

- Due diligence
- Digital authenticity
- Digital self-perception
- Digital self-evaluation

WHAT IS DIGITAL SELF-PERCEPTION, AND WHY IS IT IMPORTANT?

Digital self-perception is how you see yourself in the online environment. Being aware of who you are and understanding how your values and capabilities contribute to your online persona are essential. Your digital self-perception requires that you be honest with yourself. You have strengths as well as weaknesses. You have knowledge, skills, and abilities, but you may also have areas that need improvement. For example, you may be impatient or inflexible. Or you may participate in professional volunteer events but fail to follow through on assigned tasks. You might become aware of this deficit if your peers constantly text you with reminders to complete tasks. Everything about yourself must be identified and evaluated. Areas that require improvement should be targeted and worked on.

Why is digital self-perception important? It can help you identify and evaluate your strengths and weaknesses so that you gain a clearer and truer picture of what you represent online. Are you well qualified for the jobs you seek? Do your skills match those required by the hiring organization? An accurate appraisal of your online persona can help you get the job for which you are most qualified because prospective employers will better understand who you are in the online environment. It is incumbent on you to assist prospective employers in seeing the real you. Employers that can easily recognize the value you can bring to their organization are more likely to interview you.

YOU ARE THE CREATOR OF YOUR DIGITAL PERSONA

Evaluate yourself as you appear in the online environment. Can you easily define your skills from what you see? Can you truthfully describe your background based on what you find online? Only you know what you can do; no one else can undertake this evaluation for you. Digital mentors can assist you, but due diligence is still required on your part. This evaluation is really an inventory of your knowledge, skills, and abilities (KSAs). Do not take shortcuts here, as this is an essential step in the process of establishing your digital career path.

Action Items

1. Examine your LinkedIn profile. Are your strengths easily identifiable? Or does your profile contain vague statements?

2. Review your resume. Does it reflect healthcare knowledge and experience?

3. Analyze your Facebook, Twitter, and Instagram accounts. Can you find any evidence of competencies in areas such as leadership, finance, and communication?

4. List other online professional commitments in which you regularly participate, such as online community forums or interest groups. Do they showcase your credentials, certifications, and achievement awards?

5. Evaluate what others say about you online— for example, in LinkedIn endorsements or recommendations, social media posts, and replies to posts you have made.

The digital self-evaluation tool in exhibit 3.1 is a good starting point for the assessment process. You can add to this tool as you become more familiar with how to use it for your benefit. It can help you understand how to be more specific in describing your accomplishments, work experience, and values. The tool also maps each assessment item to goals and suggests actions you can take to achieve those goals and ensure they are visible online.

IS YOUR DIGITAL SELF-PERCEPTION REALISTIC?

Recent graduates often have more confidence in their KSAs than they have actual experience because, while in school, they had limited opportunities for assessment beyond course grades. Working during

EXHIBIT 3.1: Digital Self-Evaluation Assessment Tool

Item	Metrics	Digital goals	Actions to achieve goals and authenticity
Knowledge of healthcare	• Graduate degree and certificates • Internship experience • Work experience • Professional volunteer experience • Networking	• Present yourself online as knowledgeable to improve your career prospects. • Develop an online reputation as an expert.	• Post an up-to-date resume on LinkedIn and Facebook showcasing your degrees and relevant experience. • Use Twitter to follow and chat informally with people in healthcare.
KSAs specific to the job opening (e.g., leadership, communication, marketing skills)	• Past job accomplishments • Assigned duties and responsibilities at current job • Resume examples	• Construct a digital identity that consistently demonstrates to prospective employers and recruiters that your KSAs match their requirements.	• Review your resume to ensure it includes facts and figures. • Make sure your application contains specific, not vague, statements (e.g., "I led a six-member team").
Unstated employer qualifications (e.g., value) and determinants of successful achievements	• Organization websites • Networking • Past and current employees	• Ensure that your digital profiles demonstrate how you succeeded in various endeavors. • Explain in your online profiles how you brought value to a current or past employer.	• Ask LinkedIn mentors for opinions of an organization. • Use Facebook and Twitter to learn more about the organization and to showcase your successes. • Solicit recommendations from current coworkers and supervisors.

Category	Evidence	Digital strategy	Action items
Evidence of going above and beyond (i.e., exceeding expectations)	• Past performance reviews • Letters of reference • University transcripts • Evidence of volunteer work	• Use your digital profile to demonstrate that you are not average.	• Provide a link to a presentation you gave or the program of a conference you organized. • Quantify your achievements as much as possible.
Adaptability and flexibility	• Resume • LinkedIn endorsements • Articles or mentions in association newsletters	• Ensure your digital profile demonstrates and explains your ability to adapt and be flexible both in the workplace and in your external professional commitments.	• Review your resume to identify and record occasions on which you showed you were able to adapt to changing situations. • Submit a note or an article to an association newsletter detailing how you organized an event. • Solicit external peer reviews from LinkedIn mentors.
Maturity	• Resume • LinkedIn profile and feedback • Facebook	• Provide online evidence that you are responsible and reliable—qualities associated with adult behaviors.	• Use Facebook to provide specific examples showing your ability to stay on task until a project is completed. • Use LinkedIn to demonstrate that your expertise is advanced.
Creative thinking	• Awards • Community or professional involvement • Work achievement recognition • Scholarly recognition	• Showcase your creativity with tangibles.	• Review your resume to ensure it is up-to-date in terms of awards and similar achievements. • Update your LinkedIn profile and Facebook.

the school year, internships, and professional volunteer activities can help new graduates better assess who they truly are. Remember: No one is perfect. Most of the people who have an opportunity to evaluate your work—whether they are instructors or supervisors or professional colleagues—want you to learn, grow, and improve. They want you to succeed. Take their comments constructively.

Because of social media, many confuse digital self-perception with the online image they have created or a baseless, imagined self. All too often, job applicants project themselves as "enhanced"— they exaggerate their accomplishments on resumes, for example, or they embellish the title or duties of a previous job. Doing so not only deceives the prospective employer but also engages the applicant in self-deception, neither of which contributes to success in the job search. It also affects one's ability to find mentors among healthcare executives who have learned to detect what is real and what is not.

One survey of millennials revealed that they lie twice as much on their resumes as other adults. They also exaggerate their job titles and inflate their skills. Of the millennials who reported that they had lied on their resumes, 73 percent claimed that they didn't feel guilty about it. Furthermore, 55 percent of the millennials who lied said they would probably do it again (Corbin 2019; Rosenberg 2019).

If you get a job by falsifying your skills and pretending to be someone you aren't, you likely will be discovered—for example, when you are unable to carry out a job function, such as conducting HIPAA (Health Insurance Portability and Accountability Act) audits. If you can't do what you claimed, you may be dismissed or, at a minimum, put on probation. This will represent a significant failure and likely damage your psyche, which can set you back and negatively affect your interviewing abilities in the future. Especially in healthcare, falsifying your skills and abilities can have major implications. Healthcare organizations are human service organizations where patients' health, well-being, and lives are at stake.

One more thing: If you omit short-term jobs from your resume, employers may still find this information online. A former human resources director in healthcare, Amy White, shared that she finds it remarkable that applicants assume employers will not have time to verify their information. They do have the time, and they will check on you (Corbin 2019). Employers have a variety of online resources at their disposal, all just a click away. Larger organizations have human resources staff dedicated to verifying your information (Doyle 2019).

Action Items

1. Review your online resume and posts. Do they show you as you want to be depicted online?
2. List the qualifications and characteristics of the person you aspire to be online. Save them for career-planning goals.

HOW CAN ONLINE PEERS AND MENTORS HELP YOU GAIN A CLEARER PICTURE OF YOURSELF?

If you have limited to no work experience, mentors can help you navigate your job search. With the growth of social media and online resources such as LinkedIn, which has 530 million professionals in its online community, you now have access to a variety of executives online who can guide and advise you. Upwards of 80 percent of professionals on LinkedIn are either looking to become mentors or are searching for mentors (Jalan 2017).

To find and connect with people on LinkedIn who can advise you, do the following:

- Go to the dashboard on your LinkedIn profile.
- Locate the Career Advice hub.
- Enter your preferences for the type of advice you're seeking.

LinkedIn will recommend other members for "lightweight" mentoring based on your specifications, shared interests, and what the LinkedIn community knows about you professionally from your LinkedIn profile and activities.

Although LinkedIn mentoring relationships are not as substantial as traditional mentorships, they can still be helpful to you. Just be careful to avoid quitting the relationship if something doesn't work out after the first interaction. Go back to your online mentor and explain what happened or what went wrong. You might have missed something, and the mentor may be able to help you analyze the situation. On the other hand, if your mentor just isn't working out—if their advice is not helping you—simply thank them and move on. The following Early Careerist Case depicts a recent graduate who made the right move reaching out for online mentors.

EARLY CAREERIST CASE

Doing Something Right: Reaching Out for Online Mentors

Emily graduated two years ago with a master's degree in health services administration. Before and during graduate school, she completed two summer internships at local healthcare facilities—one a large multigroup physician practice, the other a 200-bed community hospital. Upon graduation, she accepted a position in an insurance company. However, she really wanted to acquire more experience in hospital management.

She wasn't having much luck in her job inquiries. The employment market was extremely competitive. Emily spent some time on digital self-evaluation and was convinced that her online persona was authentic. She went to LinkedIn, where she sought out online mentors by posting her interest in connecting with healthcare executives. She specifically mentioned her need for some direction in getting a job in hospital management. In response, several executives suggested that she expand her job opportunities by considering consulting firms that worked with hospitals.

Emily went online and quickly found an opening at such a consulting group. She completed the online application, a telephone interview, and then a Skype interview. Following these interviews, she received an e-mail asking her to come in for a face-to-face interview. Emily kept her online mentors informed about these developments in real time.

ARE YOU PERCEIVED AS A LEADER ONLINE?

You want prospective employers to easily understand your strengths as they relate to job opportunities. People often list "leadership" as a top job skill, but recent graduates and early careerists unfortunately tend to speak about leadership only in vague, nonspecific terms during job interviews and in professional conversations. Simply stating that you have performed as a leader is meaningless to a future boss.

Exhibit 3.2 suggests ways you can improve your chances of being perceived as a leader in the online environment. Compiling this information may require some additional work in the beginning, but it will become effortless if you make it a habit to track any and all examples of leadership.

HOW DO YOU DETERMINE IF YOU'LL FIT THE ORGANIZATION'S CULTURE?

Knowing who you are online and how others perceive you is the first step. But when applying for a job, you must also assess the organization's culture, which can be difficult to detect even if

EXHIBIT 3.2: How to Be Perceived as a Leader in the Online Environment

List examples of your leadership skills on your social media profiles.

Use technology to document your leadership activities. For example, smartphone videos of talks you give can easily be uploaded to your profile on social media, including Instagram.

Identify any leadership positions you held for a volunteer or student organization, such as a student chapter.

Note any service you performed as the chair of a panel discussion or program committee.

Indicate completion of any formal leadership training, such as that acquired in the military.

Describe leadership roles you had at volunteer events, such as food bank collections or blood drives.

Detail leadership training attended and certificates awarded. If you have photos or a video of the convocation ceremony, upload it to your social media profiles.

Describe any leadership experience you acquired in past jobs, being specific about what was involved.

you look closely. Organizational culture is reflected in the values and behaviors of the organization, such as employee attitudes toward patients and coworkers. Particularly important is upper management's behavior. You must ascertain whether you will be a good fit with the culture and, subsequently, whether the organization is a good fit for your goals and values. Too often, people assume they will just naturally work well with others or that they will share similar values because the job environment is healthcare. It is not that easy. Assessing the values of employees, customers, and organizational stakeholders is challenging. But you must determine at the outset if you perceive congruence working with them.

Do your due diligence and research the prospective employer. Examine the organization by way of its staffing. Where did key staff members work previously? What are their educational credentials? Are they involved in professional organizations? Are any of them graduates of your program? Check their LinkedIn profiles. The online environment also permits you to view the organization's website and activities, especially on Facebook pages.

Using Google, you can do research to learn more about the organization's upper management team. Twitter can allow you to follow the CEO and other senior leaders to gain more insight about the organization. Glassdoor gathers employee reviews for approximately 860,000 companies and offers insight into what it is like to work at a particular company from the employees' perspective. Salary data is usually available, too. You can also use Indeed and PayScale to access similar data and reviews.

CHAPTER SUMMARY

This chapter explored digital self-perception—how you perceive yourself online. Does how you see yourself match how others, such as employers, perceive you online? For example, do you see yourself as highly accomplished whereas others view you as someone who embellishes their resume? How do you show others that you have what it takes to do the job?

This chapter described several digital self-evaluation assessment tools you can use to establish an online persona that reflects who you really are and that demonstrates your employability. By establishing digital evaluation goals and authenticating them on online platforms such as Twitter, Facebook, Snapchat, and LinkedIn, you present a more comprehensive and realistic view of your digital persona.

This chapter also explained why you need to examine and understand who you are online to accurately present yourself to prospective employers. Undertaking a digital self-evaluation is a key step in the process of figuring out who you are online. Involving online mentors and peers in defining your persona can be helpful.

In the online environment, it's easy to embellish and exaggerate your digital persona. You must be careful not to fall into this trap.

Employers verify the information on job applications, and they can readily access information about you on social media, including Facebook posts and Twitter conversations.

This chapter recommends the following:

- Commit to seeing yourself authentically in the online environment. Digital authenticity is achievable and should be a goal.

- Look for help online. You have resources at your disposal that prior generations did not have. Digital mentoring, even lightweight, is easily accessible.

- Venture beyond the field of healthcare. For example, try one of the most wide-reaching resources, Monster.com. Monster is a global employment solution for people seeking career opportunities. The website identifies the top skills and qualifications required in health services administration, including education, technology skills, management skills, legal and regulatory knowledge, the ability to implement policy (especially as it relates to reimbursement), leadership, and an understanding of what the fundamental business of healthcare is—patient care.

- Make sure there is congruence between who you really are and the organizational values of the prospective employer. Getting the job is one thing; keeping it is another. If you are not a good fit with the organization's values, working there will be difficult, and you may end up quitting—or worse, being terminated.

- Always be aware of how the job you have helps you advance in your career. Scan your digital profile routinely to ensure you are keeping up.

- Continue to assess yourself digitally as you progress in your career. Note how you have changed online. Monitor and update your online social media accounts continuously.

- Monitor and evaluate the perceptions of your online peers and mentors. You may think you are growing in your job, but your online peers and mentors may believe otherwise.

RESOURCES

Glassdoor: www.glassdoor.com.

Indeed: www.indeed.com.

Monster: www.monster.com.

PayScale: www.payscale.com.

REFERENCES

Corbin, E. 2019. "Millennials Lie Twice as Much as Everyone Else on Their Resumes—Here's What They Lie About." Published August 6. www.gobankingrates.com/making-money/jobs/why-americans-lie-on-resumes/.

Doyle, A. 2019. "Employment History Verification." Updated August 9. www.thebalancecareers.com/employment-history-verification-2059609.

Jalan, A. 2017. "Introducing LinkedIn Career Advice, a New Way to Help You Find and Connect with Professionals for Mentorship." *LinkedIn Blog*. Published November 15. https://blog.linkedin.com/2017/november/15/introducing-linkedin-career-advice-a-new-way-to-help-you-find-and-connect.

Rosenberg, M. 2019. "Generational Names in the United States." ThoughtCo. Updated June 8. www.thoughtco.com/names-of-generations-1435472.

.

CHAPTER 4

Digital Self-Branding

DID YOU KNOW that according to a 2018 report from the US Bureau of Labor Statistics,

- the average person spends 4.2 years at a job and
- younger workers stay even less—about 2.8 years?

Or that according to Deloitte's 2019 Global Millennial Study (Ritschel 2018),

- 43 percent of millennials plan to leave their job within two years and
- only 28 percent plan to stay beyond five years?

Or that according to a 2017 national survey conducted by the Harris Poll for Career Builder (Connley 2017),

- more than half of employers (57 percent) won't hire you without an online presence;
- most employers (70 percent) will use social media to screen you, up from 11 percent in 2006; and
- more than half of employers (54 percent) will decide not to hire you because of your social media profiles?

These statistics mean that you will likely have to spend more time and effort searching for a job. They also mean that employers will be scrutinizing you more frequently online and that your social media activity holds considerable potential to influence their hiring decisions. So, in addition to filling out job applications, you would be wise to regularly update your resume and, as discussed in previous chapters, clean up your online persona. Furthermore, you should ensure your digital brand is kept up to date.

This chapter aims to help you create, modify, and monitor your digital brand. Social media play a pivotal role. Your brand is what differentiates you from others; it tells employers why you are more special than other applicants and why you deserve to be hired. You have both an offline and an online (digital) brand. Your digital brand tells the story of who you are online, which is reflected in your social media profiles and is more complex and nuanced than your offline brand. Because most employers today are screening job applicants online and are basing their hiring decisions on applicants' social media presence, creating a strong digital brand—beginning with your social media—is crucial.

CHAPTER KEYWORDS

- Offline brand
- Online (digital) brand
- Unique selling points
- Expertise

DISTINGUISHING YOUR OFFLINE AND ONLINE BRANDS

You create your brand. It is personal to you, and it evolves as you grow and change. Tangible factors such as education, professional experiences, employment, and volunteer activities all influence your brand. Intangible factors such as integrity, trust, and personality also are part of your brand, both offline and online.

Your offline brand is how you are perceived in face-to-face (F2F) situations. Your offline brand includes your physical appearance, style, personality, and behaviors that are observable in F2F situations (e.g., enthusiasm). In the past, these factors were what employers experienced during an interview. You might be hired based not only on your resume but on your personality and enthusiasm for the job.

In the online environment, the situation is different. You may not even have a F2F interview. Instead, the interview might take place via telephone or Skype, or you might not have an interview at all. Your hiring might depend solely on your digital brand to communicate who you are.

You may be unaware of the impact your digital brand has on your job search and employment efforts. Prospective employers, social media groups, and professional networks all look to your digital brand for information about you. Thus, taking control of your digital brand is imperative to ensure that the brand you show others online will be effective in your job hunt.

Did You Know?

Your digital brand begins on the first day of school with the headshot you select for your school profile or classroom avatar. Use a professional headshot that shows you in nice attire, looking like a professional (or at least an aspiring professional). Don't choose a photo that includes friends or animals or that shows you on vacation, because such photos are personal. Also, go easy on the filters. This photo is not a selfie. You want to show yourself as a professional, not a celebrity wannabe.

BRANDING YOURSELF AS A PRODUCT

Digital branding is essentially a form of marketing. Branding your-self during your job search is similar to branding a product: You are selling yourself as a product, and the potential employer is your customer. Your digital brand should differentiate you from other job candidates, who are your competitors. Focus on portraying a consistent image that demonstrates both tangible and intangible factors (Digital Marketing Institute 2020).

Examples of tangible factors include

- expertise;
- experience; and
- knowledge, skills, and abilities.

Examples of intangible factors include

- passion for your field or job,
- an ability to work well with others,
- personality,
- professional reputation,
- integrity, and
- trustworthiness.

A *social media handle* is your username preceded by the "@" symbol. Your handle is a major part of your digital self-branding. Try to use the same handle throughout your social media accounts. Create a professional and recognizable one, such as @firstnamelastname.

Action Items

1. Revisit your *professional image photo*, which is more expansive than a headshot. If you don't have one, you can create it now; a smartphone works fine, and a friend can take it for you. The photo should show you from the waist up. Wear business attire and stand in front of a neutral-color background. The photo can be cropped for use as your headshot or in your social media profiles.

2. Create an online *professional photo album* on your social media accounts. Include photos from volunteer activities, professional events, and award ceremonies.

ESTABLISHING, DEVELOPING, AND DISPLAYING EXPERTISE ON SOCIAL MEDIA

Expertise is defined as a high level of skill or knowledge (Cambridge Dictionary 2020). It is a basis of credibility. To assess your current level of healthcare expertise, answer the following questions:

- Do others perceive you to be knowledgeable in healthcare matters?
- Have you received any recognition or awards for your knowledge? For example:
  - Did your team win or place in the University of Alabama at Birmingham Health Administration Case Competition?
  - Did you receive a commendation from your local chapter of the American College of Healthcare Executives?
- Can you demonstrate training or experience in healthcare? For example:
  - Do you have a graduate degree in health services administration, public health, or a similar field?

- Have you completed any internships, or perhaps an administrative fellowship at a health system?
- Have you worked in a hospital, an insurance company, or a county government office that oversees local community health initiatives?

Expertise is an essential component of your brand, both offline and online. It is a key differentiator in presenting yourself to potential employers. Your digital brand must clearly identify your areas of professional expertise and offer proof to validate your claims. Anyone can allege expertise, but employers will want evidence. Social proof—that is, proof originating from social media—can help substantiate your expertise (Bullas 2020).

To figure out if you have sufficient *demonstrated expertise* to brand yourself professionally as an expert, make a table with two columns. In the first column, identify your perceived areas of expertise. If necessary, consult past job descriptions and resumes, or ask your work colleagues and peers for input. In the other column, include your evidence or social proof for that area of expertise. Exhibit 4.1 presents some examples of identified expertise along with social proof for that area of expertise.

EXHIBIT 4.1: Examples of Expertise and Social Proof

Examples of expertise	Examples of social proof
Knowledge of risk management	Share content that you have authored and posted in one of your social media groups (e.g., Facebook).
Experience in organizing physician small-group conferences	Share content from LinkedIn in which you posted information about the conferences you organized. Include feedback that was posted about you and the conferences.
Ability to work well with others	Use your employer's Facebook account to provide an example of an award you received for a team project.

What do you do if you realize you are not yet an expert? One option is to concentrate on showing that you are currently working to become an expert. For example:

- List seminars that you have taken or classes in which you're currently enrolled.
- Identify any online mentors or social groups that offer support for your developing expertise. Include any comments they've shared or posted about you.
- If you are in the process of obtaining certification, indicate where you are in this process. Be specific and give details. For example, provide a link to the certification agency, highlight the certification criteria, and state your expected date of completion. If you have taken two courses and two remain, indicate which ones they are and when you will complete them.

You can also use social media to *develop* expertise. Social media groups exist for specific industries and topics, including healthcare. You can search Facebook and LinkedIn topics by using each network's search bar to find and join groups that offer you an opportunity to gain expertise. Members of these groups share information and insights that can help you build authority around your digital brand. However, be aware that some groups may be overcrowded—often with your competitors. Smaller topic-based groups may be more productive in terms of reaching an audience that will be useful to you (Digital Marketing Institute 2020).

Volunteering also can help you develop expertise and gain recognition as an expert in your field (Doyle 2019). Volunteer strategically. If you are attempting to establish expertise in public health, for example, volunteer at a local public health department or work on a research project with a public health professor at a local or even a national online university.

Display all evidence of your expertise in the online environment. Twitter, LinkedIn, and Facebook are your default social networks. Within those networks are specific industry groups and special interest topic groups. Use them to document the achievements that support your claims of expertise. Make sure to regularly post items that demonstrate you have or are gaining expertise (Bullas 2020).

Use Instagram to showcase your attendance at conferences, especially if you made a presentation. Post photos and videos of volunteer work and anything else you consider relevant. Ask work colleagues, mentors, and peers to review your postings. Get constructive feedback from them and use it.

IDENTIFYING YOUR UNIQUE SELLING POINTS

Unique selling points (USPs) are key to digital branding. Your USPs demonstrate what is exceptional about you; they identify the skills, knowledge, and experience that you possess but other applicants don't. They also include your values, characteristics, and anything else that you perceive to be distinctive and ultimately important to a prospective employer.

Make a list of your USPs. The following questions may help you identify them:

- Do you have volunteer experience?
- Did you complete an internship or a fellowship?
- Do you have international work experience?
- Do you speak another language? Do you know sign language?
- Do you regularly attend webinars to update your skills?
- Do you know how to write code or computer programs?
- Did you ever create an app for a course assignment?

Which items on your list distinguish you from other job applicants? If you are not able to identify which ones make you special, think about combinations of items. A unique combination of skills, knowledge, and experiences can set you apart too (Ball 2020).

Figuring out what makes you unique requires reflection on your part. You must think honestly and critically. Look at your resume, employee evaluations such as annual performance reviews and verbal feedback, and social media accounts. Has anyone commented on your exceptional skills or professional demeanor? Ask mentors for help here. Your peers may avoid giving you candid feedback about your USPs because they are potential competitors, whereas mentors have expertise in evaluating applicants from their own hiring experiences.

Remember that every USP promises an employer a deliverable. For example, suppose you identify service excellence as a USP. When you apply for a job at a hospital, check to see if this USP aligns with the facility's customer service goals. If so, highlight the match to the employer (Taylor 2012).

Action Items

List five of your USPs. Then consider the following questions:

1. Can you adapt this list of USPs to individual job applications?
2. Does your list tell prospective employers how perfect you are for the job?
3. Does the list tell prospective employers who you really are?

As with expertise, you must provide evidence or social proof to support your USPs:

- Do you have social proof? If yes, which of your social media accounts offer documentation?
- Is this social proof easily accessible, or are passwords required?
- Do you use Instagram to display awards or other recognitions?
- Do you use Twitter to share mentions in local news media or on professional blogs?
- Do you maintain an online blog? If not, you can create a blog with links to topic groups on social media that authenticate your knowledge and awareness of trends in healthcare.
- Do you post links on LinkedIn to online posts or publications that demonstrate your writing abilities?
- Do you showcase the number of followers you have on social networks as a means of demonstrating current and growing influence in the healthcare field?

Remember that the extent to which your content is shared, including on Twitter, LinkedIn, Instagram, and Facebook, quantifies the amount of social attention you enjoy. In so doing, it affirms the reliability of your digital brand, which can be important to employers (Bullas 2020).

CHECKLIST OF BASIC COMPONENTS OF DIGITAL BRANDING

Digital branding has several basic components. Each must be considered when developing your digital brand. Use the following checklist to guide your digital branding process.

Digital Brand Identity

Your digital brand identity demonstrates your individuality. It includes those features of your brand that create awareness about you. Creating a digital brand identity may be as simple as creating a hashtag (a metadata tag introduced by the "#" symbol) that you use or as complex as a personal branding statement (a summary of who you are) that you post on LinkedIn.

Digital Brand Integration

Digital brand integration involves ensuring that your resume, social media accounts, job applications, and professional networks all reflect your digital brand. Integration is essential because all communication must be in sync with your digital brand. Your digital brand must be consistent across all of the platforms you use for professional purposes, such as LinkedIn, Facebook, Twitter, and Instagram (Ball 2020). Employers look for consistency, so make sure your LinkedIn postings do not contradict your resume or Facebook pages.

Digital Brand Equity

Digital brand equity is the added value that is conferred on your digital brand through your social media activity, professional networks, and other online associations or relationships. For example, your value increases if you are a member of a selective social media healthcare group or have been inducted into a professional society.

Co-branding

Co-branding is the marketing of an organization's name alongside the name of another brand. This marketing strategy is believed to create synergies, where the total effect produced is greater than the effect each organization would enjoy individually. Co-branding is usually undertaken for reputational enhancement. If you work or collaborate with someone who has a well-known digital brand, you may be able to co-brand and enjoy such synergies. Try partnering with that person on a special project, such as raising funds for a local hospital or leading a volunteer group.

EARLY CAREERIST CASE

A Digital Branding Mistake: Overlooking What Makes You Stand Out

Luis was about to graduate from a master's degree program in health services administration. He was proud of the fact that he had worked his way through both college and graduate school, working part-time at a local auto dealership. While there, he had spent a great deal of time performing digital market research for the dealership. Luis's employer was so pleased with his initiative and performance that it offered him a lucrative, full-time position upon graduation as director of market research.

Even though Luis had studied branding in his marketing class, he was unaware that he had a brand and how significantly it had changed with the acquisition of digital market research skills. These research skills were differentiators. Luis wanted a healthcare internship but hadn't been very successful with his applications. One evening, he found himself walking out of the classroom with his marketing professor. He shared how his digital market research efforts had helped improve sales for the auto dealership, but he admitted he didn't want to work there forever. As Luis explained it, he was afraid that because his only employment was at an auto dealership, he wouldn't be an attractive candidate for a healthcare internship or a healthcare job.

The professor recommended that Luis think about his brand: He possessed digital market research skills and experience that could differentiate him from other applicants applying for internships. The professor encouraged Luis to think in terms of how his digital market research skills could be applied in a healthcare facility, such as a hospital. She suggested that Luis frame his interest in internships in terms of the potential value his digital market research experience and skills might represent to an organization.

Luis went home and began to reevaluate how he presented himself, especially online. He realized his digital brand did not currently reflect his unique skills in using data analytics for market research. Furthermore, he had not yet shared information about his new skills on social media. Thus, his digital brand didn't reflect how he was special.

Luis updated his resume, his social media profiles, his professional networks, and his internship applications. He made sure all items clearly reflected his expertise and experience in using data analytics for market research. Now when he submitted applications for internships, he was successful in securing interviews, both online and offline. In the end, he was offered multiple internships. It turned out that healthcare organizations were very much interested in his digital market research skills.

MONITORING AND EVALUATING YOUR DIGITAL BRAND

Monitoring and evaluating your digital brand are essential if you are to maintain control of it. You need to ensure consistency between who you are online and how others view you, especially employers. This can occur only through oversight (Brand Yourself 2020).

Working on your digital brand is a continuous process. You must monitor your brand frequently for brand effectiveness. For example, if you find that you aren't generating much interest on social media or getting many responses to your job applications, you may need to identify and address deficiencies in your brand (Doyle 2019). Consider the following questions:

- Does your digital brand still differentiate you from others?
- If so, how can you differentiate yourself even more?
- Are you diluting your brand—for example, by joining too many social media groups?

If you discover that your brand is no longer effective in differentiating you from your competitors—other job applicants—you must make changes. Start by asking yourself why you believe that your current attempts at differentiation aren't successful. What more could you do to differentiate your brand? Ask a work colleague to review your digital brand. Perhaps your brand doesn't reflect what is special about you. Identify some of your competitors and attempt to identify their digital brands. How do you compare? What can you do to extend your digital brand's positive image?

DIGITAL BRAND PERFORMANCE ASSESSMENT METRICS

Evaluating brand performance is not easy, but you can establish metrics for doing so. Brand performance metrics can be episodic or continuous; exhibit 4.2 presents examples of metrics you can use and their associated outcomes. As this table shows, brand performance metrics must be carefully evaluated because landing a job does not necessarily indicate an effective digital brand. You may have been number five on the list, and those above you declined their offers. On the other hand, perhaps your digital brand did convince the employer that you should be offered the job.

EXHIBIT 4.2: Examples of Metrics for Brand Performance and Associated Outcomes

Metric for brand performance	Associated outcome(s)
You got the job.	Your brand may be working. On the other hand, brand performance may be skewed if the top candidates took other positions or were otherwise unavailable.
Your current employer shows confidence in you.	Confidence in you can be assessed by positive annual reviews, salary increases, or promotions.
Your social media networks are growing.	Growth can be measured by additions to your social media networks, including notable experts in healthcare.
You're becoming an influencer.	The influence you have on others might be assessed by the number of conference attendees retweeting your comments or a substantial increase in the number of your followers.

DIGITAL REBRANDING AND RECOVERY STRATEGIES

If brand performance metrics suggest that your current digital brand is not working, then you need to engage in rebranding. *Rebranding* is changing your image with the intention of developing a new, differentiated identity. It can include the acquisition of new skills or updating current ones. For example, learning another language can rebrand you as having potential for global employment.

Digital brand recovery is a type of rebranding. If something occurs that negatively affects your brand, then you need to rebrand. For example, if you worked for an organization that gained notoriety for fraudulent billing practices or other illegal and unethical behaviors, your digital brand could be affected—especially if you associated yourself with your employer on Facebook, LinkedIn, or Instagram.

Some people might look for and find another job and omit their time with this employer from their resume. But as we know from previous chapters, employers can uncover such omissions and likely won't view them positively.

If you decide to stay at your current job, recover from negative fallout by cleaning up your online presence and eliminating any posts shared online that associated you with the unethical employer. Furthermore, post positively: Make sure your online posts share what is being done in terms of institutional recovery. Has the CEO stepped down or been fired? Is the board reorganizing? Update your social media accounts regularly to share any additional positive actions that are being taken.

EXTENDING BRAND IMAGE THROUGH INFLUENCERS

There is a growing segment online called *influencers*. These are individuals who have many followers and to whom people pay attention.

Connecting and collaborating with influencers is an effective way to get your digital brand known. LinkedIn is a great place to find and engage with experts in a variety of industries, including healthcare (Digital Marketing Institute 2020). However, you must spend time developing relationships with influencers. Influencers often do not appreciate uninvited relationships, so you may need to first establish yourself online and show that you deserve the relationship.

The internet makes it easy to reach out and connect with people—especially on social media. Not everyone will want that connection, nor will they want a parasitic relationship. Yes, you are new to the field, and wouldn't it be great if you could show prospective employers that you are connected to healthcare vice presidents and CEOs? Practice some restraint in trying to enhance your reputation through online associations. Not everyone wants to hook up with you.

Action Items

1. Identify top influencers in healthcare.
2. Pinpoint their areas of expertise.
3. Look at their networks, posting habits, and recent shares.
4. Reflect on how the influencers respond to what others have posted.
5. Discern best practices from their branding strategies.

CHAPTER SUMMARY

Digital self-branding is important because it can help you gain a competitive advantage in the job marketplace. Your digital brand distinguishes you from other job applicants. It also helps prospective employers discover in what ways you are different from your competitors. Your digital brand shows employers that you are a good fit with their organization and its workers. In addition, your digital brand communicates that you can add value to the organization.

Creating your digital brand is personal to you. It must be done by you. A fair number of resources are available, some of which are included in the Resources section at the end of this chapter. Ultimately, you are responsible for figuring out how you want to present yourself online. Digital branding is a continuous endeavor; you must ensure that your social media profiles are kept up to date and that you stay in touch with your online contacts. It is incumbent on you to post comments on other people's blogs, to write articles, and to attend meetings, conventions, and events in your field (Doyle 2019).

Digital Branding Checklist

1. Assume responsibility and control of your digital brand.
2. Review your USPs routinely to determine if they require any changes.
3. Update your digital brand frequently. Be sure to specifically identify any new professional goal achievements, such as earning a risk management certificate or completing a leadership course.
4. Ensure that your digital brand reflects active participation in your social media and professional networks.
5. Manage your digital brand through evaluation, monitoring, and feedback.

RESOURCES

AIM Social Media Marketing. "The Importance of Having Consistent Social Media Handles." https://aimsmmarketing.com/consistent-social-media-handles/.

Deloitte. "The Deloitte Global Millennial Survey 2019." www2.deloitte.com/global/en/pages/about-deloitte/articles/millennialsurvey.html.

REFERENCES

Ball, J. 2020. "8 Tips for Developing a Killer Personal USP (That'll Get You the Job You Deserve!)." Coburg Banks. Accessed January 6. www.coburgbanks.co.uk/blog/candidate-tips/8-tips-to-developing-a-killer-usp/.

Brand Yourself. 2020. "The Definitive Guide to Personal Branding." Accessed January 6. https://brandyourself.com/definitive-guide-to-personal-branding.

Bullas, J. 2020. "The 10 Pillars to Creating a Personal Brand in a Digital World." Accessed January 6. www.jeffbullas.com/the-10-pillars-to-creating-a-personal-brand-in-a-digital-world/.

Cambridge Dictionary. 2020. "Expertise." Accessed January 6. https://dictionary.cambridge.org/us/dictionary/english/expertise.

Connley, C. 2017. "More Than Half of Employers Won't Hire Someone They Can't Find Online." CNBC. Published August 18. www.cnbc.com/2017/08/18/more-than-half-of-employers-wont-hire-someone-they-cant-find-online.html.

Digital Marketing Institute. 2020. "10 Steps to Building Your Personal Brand on Social Media." Accessed January 6. https://digitalmarketinginstitute.com/en-au/blog/10-steps-to-building-your-personal-brand-on-social-media.

Doyle, A. 2019. "How to Create a Professional Brand." The Balance Careers. Updated January 15. www.thebalancecareers.com/how-to-create-a-professional-brand-2059761.

Ritschel, C. 2018. "Nearly Half of Millennials Plan to Leave a Job Within Two Years, Study Finds." *Independent*. Published May 21. www.independent.co.uk/life-style/millennials-jobs-career-work-salary-quit-young-people-study-a8361936.html.

Taylor, L. 2012. "How to Land the Job. Use Your Unique Selling Proposition to Stand Out from the Crowd." *Psychology Today*. Published April 11. www.psychologytoday.com/us/blog/tame-your-terrible-office-tyrant/201204/how-land-the-job.

US Bureau of Labor Statistics. 2018. "Employee Tenure Summary." Published September 20. www.bls.gov/news.release/tenure.nr0.htm.

CHAPTER 5

Self-Determined Career

When looking for a job, you usually have something in mind. In some instances—for example, when you are a recent graduate or unemployed—you may consider any healthcare position, but you still have an ultimate career goal. As mentioned in chapter 2, it is unlikely you will become a CEO immediately after graduation without any experience, but you *can* begin planning your self-determined career now. (In fact, you already started doing this when you decided to pursue a healthcare degree.)

Consider the following questions:

- Do you want to be a hospital CEO?
- Do you want to be a nursing home administrator?
- Do you want to be a data analyst for a health insurance company?
- Do you want to be a medical coder?
- Do you want to be a healthcare finance manager?

Once you establish your career plan, you can start mapping the goals needed to achieve it. So, grab your career goals from chapter 2, because you'll need them here!

WHAT IS A SELF-DETERMINED CAREER?

There are many reasons people choose careers: parents, friends, money, life experiences, hobbies, interests, passion, purpose, and more. Regardless of your reasons for choosing healthcare as a career, *you* are the major influencer of your career. *Self-determination* is the power to make decisions for yourself (Cambridge Dictionary 2020), so your self-determined career refers to your own power to make decisions related to your career. You can be assertive and proactive in seeking the job roles you want.

A self-determined career starts with two basic steps: (1) regularly reviewing job postings and descriptions and (2) creating a three-year plan that maps goals to achieve what you want.

REGULARLY REVIEW JOB POSTINGS AND DESCRIPTIONS

People usually look at job descriptions when they're hunting for a job, but you should always scan the job market even when you aren't looking for a new job. Job postings are a great way to see what is changing in the job requirements and market trends for healthcare. For example, the number of data-related or information technology jobs in healthcare is on the rise, no doubt because of the increased use of electronic health records, electronic reporting to regulatory agencies such as the National Committee for Quality Assurance, and cybersecurity threats. You can learn a lot from a job posting. You can see the requirements for education, certifications, and skills, as well as the job's responsibilities.

Conducting an internet search takes skill (see chapter 1), and this applies to searching for jobs on online job boards. Following are some tips.

Search Terms

When searching online job boards, use broader terms initially to capture more jobs. If you're looking for a job in healthcare leadership, for example, start with *health director* instead of *chief executive officer*. Using the search term *health director* will generate more job postings for different levels of healthcare management and leadership. You can search large job aggregators such as Indeed.com, as well as healthcare-specific job boards such as the American College of Healthcare Executives (ACHE) Job Center or the Public Health Jobs board managed by the Association of Schools and Programs of Public Health. You can also search the career webpages of individual healthcare organizations.

Exhibit 5.1 lists some examples of search terms and job boards. You should search at least a few job boards when regularly scanning for new job postings.

Location

If you want to look for job postings anywhere, then leave the location field empty when conducting your search. If you are looking for jobs in a specific city or state, then include it in the location field.

EXHIBIT 5.1: Examples of Search Terms and Job Boards

Search terms	Job boards— general	Job boards— healthcare
Health	CareerBuilder	ACHE Job Center
Health administration	Glassdoor	Health eCareers
Health data	Google	Hospital Careers
Health director	Indeed	Hospital Jobs
Health manager	Jobs2Careers	Hospital Jobs Online
Health policy	LinkedIn	Nurse.com Jobs
Healthcare	Monster	Nursing Jobs
Healthcare finance	SimplyHired	Public Health Jobs
Population health	USAJOBS	Public Health Employment
Public health	ZipRecruiter	Connection

Note: Job board URLs are provided in the Resources section at the end of the chapter.

WHAT TO LOOK FOR IN JOB POSTINGS AND JOB DESCRIPTIONS

Job postings and job descriptions tend to follow a general template, although you will see variations. Most include a job title, job responsibilities, job skills, and job requirements or qualifications.

Job Title

The header in the job board search listing is typically the job title. You must read beyond the job title, however, because it doesn't always describe the job fully. And sometimes the listed job title is different from the functioning title.

Job Responsibilities

The job responsibilities are what you will be doing in the job position. This section is important because it gives you insight into the job's role and essential functions, as well as the expectations of the employer. Although many job postings do not state the salary, the job responsibilities section may provide enough information to allow you to determine a fair market salary range based on other jobs with similar responsibilities and criteria.

Job Skills

The job posting may have a separate section for job skills, or they may be included among the job requirements or job qualifications. These skills are what you need to be successful in the position. Some skills may be required before you apply, while others may be learned on the job or required within a certain time frame (e.g., within six months of hire).

Job Requirements or Qualifications

Most job postings include a section for job qualifications. These are the qualifications the ideal candidate will possess. They may include education, certifications and licenses, job skills, and previous experience. You'll likely see qualifications in this section described as "required" or "preferred." Required qualifications are the ones you must possess to be considered for the position. Preferred qualifications are those that the organization's hiring manager desires but aren't strictly necessary for a candidate to be hired. Preferred qualifications are usually related to the specific position. Possessing both the required and preferred qualifications will make you a top applicant for the position.

- **Education:** Most positions have an educational requirement. For many healthcare positions, you will meet this requirement if you have a health degree. However, positions for some specialties may have more specific requirements.

- **Certifications and licenses:** Healthcare is heavily regulated—as it should be, given that we are responsible for the lives and well-being of our patients. Many certifications and licenses are relevant in healthcare, and these vary by specialty. For example, there are clinical licenses (e.g., for nurses and physicians), technical certifications (e.g., medical coding, health information management), and professional certifications (e.g., leadership, finance). You'll have to become familiar with what is needed for your career path. Job postings usually list the certifications and licenses required, if any.

- **Job skills:** Required job skills can include both hard and soft skills. Examples of hard skills include typing speed and experience with computer software programs such as Microsoft Office. Soft skills may include the ability to communicate and manage your time well. You can develop many job skills through self-learning (see chapter 6) to advance your healthcare career.

- **Previous experience:** In many job postings, the job requirements or qualifications section includes content related to experience acquired in previous positions. Pay attention to this information, because it can help you design your career path. For example, a vice president of operations position may require experience at the director level, and a director of patient care services may need several years of nursing management experience. If your goal is to be a vice president of operations, you need to include these other positions in your career path.

> **Action Items**
>
> 1. Pick two job boards and two job search terms. Search each term on each job board. For each search, review five job postings (20 job postings in all).
> 2. In the job postings you review, find the job responsibilities and job qualifications and study them.

CREATE A THREE-YEAR CAREER PLAN

You're often encouraged to think of your career as part of your lifelong plan, but so many unpredictable events can affect your goals—marriage, relocation, and layoffs, to name just a few. Your goals and what you want to achieve will likely change as a result of these events. Therefore, a good approach is to create a plan that outlines your goals for three years. A three-year period is manageable and more foreseeable than 20 years.

When you create your three-year plan, be sure to consider different aspects of your career. Money is one aspect, but your three-year career plan shouldn't emphasize only money or salary. Instead, focus on your job aspirations and the skills you need to achieve them:

- Are any certifications or licenses required?
- What job skills do you need to build?
- What job experience do you need to acquire?

Certifications and Licenses

At the beginning of this chapter, did you answer yes to the question "Do you want to be a hospital CEO?" If so, you'll probably want to become a Fellow of the American College of Healthcare Executives (FACHE), because the FACHE credential indicates board certification in healthcare leadership. Many other healthcare certifications are available, and it's important to identify the ones relevant to your career path. Most certifications require an exam and continuing education, both of which entail certain fees and costs. Quality is more important than quantity, so resist the lure of obtaining too many certifications. Understanding the certifications that are beneficial to your career path will allow you to pursue the ones with the greatest value.

Here are examples of the certifications and licenses that are needed for various healthcare positions:

- Fellow of the American College of Healthcare Executives (FACHE)
- Certified Health Education Specialist (CHES)
- Certified Healthcare Environmental Services Professional (CHESP)
- Certified Healthcare Facility Manager (CHFM)
- Certified Healthcare Financial Professional (CHFP)
- Certified in Healthcare Human Resources (CHHR)
- Certified Professional in Healthcare Information and Management Systems (CPHIMS)
- Certified Professional in Healthcare Quality (CPHQ)
- Certified Professional in Healthcare Risk Management (CPHRM)
- Certified Professional in Patient Safety (CPPS)
- Certified in Public Health (CPH)
- Clinical licenses (e.g., RN, MD, PT, EMT)
- IASSC Certified Lean Six Sigma Black Belt (ICBB)
- Professional, Academy for Healthcare Management (PAHM)
- Project Management Professional (PMP)

Job Skills

Understanding your strengths and weaknesses is vital (see chapter 2), but so is knowing the skill set you've acquired from school coursework and past work experience. If you can identify which job skills you already possess, you can determine which ones you still need to acquire to advance your healthcare career. Paying close attention to the job skills listed in the job descriptions for the types of positions you want will guide your path in developing new skills.

Job Positions

As noted earlier, if you want to be a vice president of operations, then you need to include a director-level position in your career mapping. As part of your regular review of current job postings, study any director-level positions you encounter to see what prior work experience those jobs require, and add other necessary job positions to your career map.

MAPPING GOALS AND OBJECTIVES TO YOUR THREE-YEAR PLAN

Knowing *what* you want to accomplish in the next three years is your career *plan*, but *how* you will accomplish it is your career *map*. To achieve your plan, you must map goals to each year and objectives to each goal. Reevaluate your goals and objectives each year to determine your progress and adjust them as needed. Your three-year career plan isn't permanent, so you can modify it anytime. If you finish one goal early or get a promotion that wasn't in your original plan, you can adjust your goals and objectives for the subsequent years.

Exhibit 5.2 shows a sample three-year plan with mapped goals and objectives.

EXHIBIT 5.2: Sample Three-Year Career Plan and Map

Year 1

Improve professional network.

- Create a LinkedIn profile.
- Invite healthcare professionals to connect.
- Attend three local networking events.

Year 2

Improve leadership skills.

- Volunteer with a community organization.
- Ask to lead a project or workshop at the volunteer organization or at work.

Get a healthcare job (if not already employed in healthcare).

- Apply for at least five positions each week.
- Update resume.

Year 3

Complete certification.

- Study for the certification exam.
- Take the exam.

Improve leadership skills.

- Find a mentor or shadow a healthcare executive.
- Participate in leadership training.

Become a better writer.

- Write in a journal at least three times a week.

Reevaluate goals and objectives, and assess the progress achieved.

Action Items

1. Identify job skills or certifications that you need to advance on the career path you have chosen.

2. Identify three to five career goals that you want to accomplish over the next three years.

3. Determine how you will achieve those goals by creating at least one objective for each.

4. Create a timeline for your goals and objectives. Which ones can you accomplish in year 1 of your career plan? Which ones can you accomplish in years 2 and 3?

CHAPTER SUMMARY

Having a career plan will help you achieve your goals. After all, as French writer Antoine de Saint-Exupéry said, "A goal without a plan is just a wish" (Gordon 2012). *You* are the major influencer in your career to get the healthcare jobs you want. So be assertive and proactive with your self-determined career.

RESOURCES

Job Boards—General

CareerBuilder: www.careerbuilder.com.

Glassdoor: www.glassdoor.com.

Google: www.google.com (general search engine for job search terms).

Indeed: www.indeed.com.

Jobs2Careers: www.jobs2careers.com.

LinkedIn: www.linkedin.com.

Monster: www.monster.com.

SimplyHired: www.simplyhired.com.

USAJOBS: www.usajobs.gov.

ZipRecruiter: www.ziprecruiter.com.

Job Boards—Healthcare

ACHE Job Center (member log-in required): www.ache.org/career-resource-center/job-center.

Health eCareers: www.healthecareers.com.

Hospital Careers: www.hospitalcareers.com.

Hospital Jobs: https://hospitaljobs.com.

Hospital Jobs Online: www.hospitaljobsonline.com.

Nurse.com Jobs: www.nurse.com/jobs.

Nursing Jobs: www.nursingjobs.com.

Public Health Jobs: https://publichealthjobs.org.

Public Health Employment Connection: https://apps.sph.emory. edu/PHEC/.

REFERENCES

Cambridge Dictionary. 2020. "Self-Determination." Accessed January 10. https://dictionary.cambridge.org/us/dictionary/english/ self-determination.

Gordon, J. 2012. "Planning for Success: 'A Goal Without a Plan Is Just a Wish.'—Antoine de Saint-Exupery." Published May 14. https://theproblem-solver.com/planning-for-success-a-goal-without-a-plan-is-just-a-wish-antoine-de-saint-exupery/.

CHAPTER 6

Self-Learning

Learning should not stop after you graduate. Being a life-long learner is critical to your success. Many of the top professionals you read about demonstrate this philosophy: Warren Buffett, Bill Gates, and Oprah Winfrey are just a few examples of those who have expressed their dedication to continued learning. Business magnate Elon Musk read multiple books to learn about rockets before he founded aerospace manufacturing company SpaceX (Cantrell 2014).

During your healthcare career, you can gain new skills not only through experience but also through self-learning. If you have recently graduated, learning is probably the last thing you want to do! But before long, you will again be ready to learn new skills that will enhance your career. Continually learning new skills will also help you keep up with the changing healthcare environment.

CHAPTER KEYWORDS

- Self-learning
- Skill building
- Online resources

MAKE LEARNING NEW JOB SKILLS A PRIORITY

You should evaluate your skills frequently and identify how you can improve them. Although money and education are important considerations in your career decisions, learning new skills may have a greater impact on your career advancement (which often leads to a higher salary). While it is ideal to learn new job skills in a healthcare organization, you can gain valuable skills in other industries, too. You can learn customer service in retail and hospitality, for example, or money handling and accounting as a cashier. The value of learning from other industries is demonstrated by hospitals that have adapted Disney World's customer experience principles to improve their patient experience (Doughman 2011).

Based on everything you have read in this book so far, what do you need to learn to become a better healthcare professional and advance your career?

- Do you need leadership skills?
- Do you need to improve your written communication?
- Do you need a more advanced working knowledge of Microsoft Office programs such as Excel or Access?
- Do you need to improve your understanding of biostatistics?
- Do you want to learn project management methodology?
- Do you want to become more culturally competent?
- Do you need to increase your typing speed?
- Do you need to learn how to use a numeric keypad for data entry or accounting?
- Do you want to learn Lean Six Sigma principles?
- Do you want to learn about emergency preparedness and disaster management?

Once you have determined the skills you need, you can begin self-learning and using the online resources available to you.

ONLINE AND DIGITAL RESOURCES FOR LEARNING NEW SKILLS

There are many online and digital resources that can help you develop new job skills. The internet makes so much information immediately accessible, and a lot of it is available at no cost to you.

Online Videos

Through the many videos on sites such as YouTube and Vimeo, you can learn numerous new skills. You can improve your skills in data analysis, disaster preparedness, healthcare quality, and so much more. You can watch TED Talks by top healthcare executives or videos from well-known healthcare organizations such as the Agency for Healthcare Research and Quality.

Online Articles and Blogs

Online articles and blogs are a great source for new information on healthcare trends. You can read scientific research articles in peer-reviewed journals and the latest news on blogs. Although access to most scientific journals is available only through membership or subscription, some journals publish open-access articles. Many universities and healthcare organizations provide useful information on online blogs. Of course, it's important to make sure a blog is credible and not just the top gossip column. To find credible resources, start by looking at regulatory health agencies (e.g., the Joint Commission, Centers for Medicare & Medicaid Services), health organizations (American Heart Association, American Diabetes Association), professional health organizations (American Hospital Association, Clinical Social Work Association), and local health departments and hospitals.

Podcasts

Podcasts are the new radio or TV talk shows. They are easy to access through your computer or smartphone, and you can listen to them during your commute to work. One great thing about podcasts is that they give you an opportunity to learn about various health specialties without needing to schedule a meeting. You can learn about health information technology (IT), patient engagement, health policy, or healthcare cybersecurity. The length of podcasts can be as short as two minutes or as long as an hour, so you can tailor your podcast viewing according to your schedule or commute time.

Online Training

Online training is a good way to learn new skills in a structured format. This mode of education may feel familiar if you took college courses online or computer-based training at work. Online training can be free or paid, and both may count toward the continuing education requirements you need to fulfill for certain health certifications. Many professional health organizations offer online training opportunities.

E-books and Digital Magazines

Reading will always be one of the best ways to learn, but carrying hard copies is not always practical. Having electronic access to periodicals and books (including audio books) creates more opportunities to learn. If you get stuck waiting longer than expected for an appointment, for example, or if a meeting finishes 10 minutes early, you can pull out your smartphone or reading device and get in a little more learning. Many e-books you will have to pay for, but free ones are available. For example, Amazon offers many free e-books, including health-related titles. You can also borrow e-books from your public library.

Hands-On Practice

Reading, listening, and studying are all ways to learn, but actually *doing*—that is, hands-on practice—is very helpful. You can really enhance your technical or writing skills in a digital environment. You can improve your typing speed and accuracy using online typing tests (very helpful if you are currently a two-finger typist), create mock presentations and infographics, or draft an article for a health blog. You can also access online simulations to improve your interviewing skills or medical decision-making.

University Alumni Resources

If you attended a college or university, you may have resources available to you through your alma mater. As an alum, you may still have access to your university library's online holdings, where you can access reading material (including subscription-based research journals), career services, and online training courses. Contact your university's alumni association to see what is available to you.

CONSIDER EARNING RELEVANT CERTIFICATIONS

In chapter 5, we discussed certifications and provided some examples. Healthcare has many certifications, which is to be expected in such a highly regulated industry. Certifications let employers and patients know that you meet a certain level of competency in that specialty. But certification often requires an exam and continuing education, both of which entail various costs and fees. Some certifications also require a certain number of years' experience or membership before you are even eligible to apply.

When you looked at job positions you might be interested in, did you see any consistency in terms of certifications? For example, if you want to work in risk management or regulatory compliance, you may have seen required job qualifications that included certifications such as CPHRM (Certified Professional in Healthcare Risk Management), CPPS (Certified Professional in Patient Safety), CPHQ (Certified Professional in Healthcare Quality), or Lean and Six Sigma process improvement.

You should have noted any required certifications in your three-year career plan. You can visit the certifying agency's website and read the eligibility requirements there. Work toward only one certification at a time. Choose the most important one and add it to your career map. Then start studying and self-learning for your certification exam.

READ! READ! READ!

The saying "It's not rocket science!" implies that aerospace engineering is the most complex subject to learn (Martin 2019). Yet, as mentioned earlier, Elon Musk was able to learn rocket science by reading about it and is now making history in America's space program. We read every day—text messages, e-mails, and social media posts, for example. But *what* we read can have a major impact on our lives and career.

Reading allows you to learn, grow, and expand your knowledge without the need to travel anywhere or spend a lot of money. Healthcare professionals may specialize in finance, law, billing, or environmental services, but influential healthcare professionals and leaders understand how the many different areas of healthcare operate and interconnect.

Understanding the roles and responsibilities of each area will enhance your abilities as a healthcare leader. So, learn about nursing, emergency management, logistics, health insurance, trending health topics, new health technology, and health policies affecting your community. Read real-life stories, case studies, impact reports, white papers, brochures, and presentation slides. Even if you recognize misinformation in what you read, it can help you identify what others may hear or see so that you can respond as needed.

> To learn more about trends in healthcare, read the following periodicals regularly:
>
> - *Modern Healthcare*
> - *Healthcare Executive*
> - *Becker's Hospital Review*

BEFORE GOING BACK TO SCHOOL—STOP!

An education gives you a tremendous advantage—your degree will prove invaluable in your healthcare career. But more than one degree won't necessarily advance your healthcare career unless a job requires it. For example, say you have a master's in health services administration but you want to be a paramedic. You will never get a job as a paramedic without completing the necessary schooling. The same applies to most clinical professions.

If you have a degree—especially a master's degree—then building your skills and experience will be more effective in advancing your career than going back to school. However, if you truly want to get another degree, then do so only if it doesn't require taking on new debt. If your employer has a tuition program, use it. You can gain experience and develop your skills by taking one or two classes at a time.

Consider the following questions to help you decide if you should go back to school:

- Do you truly need it for your career?
- Can you do it without taking on new debt?
- Is it the only way to learn the subject—you can't learn it through self-learning, reading, or certifications?

If you answered no to any of these questions, then going back to school may not be the best option. You need to explore all of your options carefully and reconsider the best route to learn new skills.

If you have a degree and do decide to go back to school, your previous coursework may apply toward a second degree. Most universities impose restrictions on transfer credits, however, so be sure to maximize the number of courses applied to your next degree. If you are an alum, your university will likely honor most of your previous credit hours so that you don't need to repeat courses to fulfill general education requirements.

Action Items

Complete at least three items from the list below:

1. Find and watch one online video related to healthcare leadership.
2. Read at least one online article on a current health topic.
3. Complete an online FEMA (Federal Emergency Management Agency) training certificate, such as IS-100.C (https://training.fema.gov/is/crslist.aspx).
4. Learn how to create a frequency distribution and histogram using Microsoft Excel (www.youtube.com/watch?v=kEHa-NkZDV4).
5. Take a typing test or a numeric keyboard test (https://official-typing-test.com).

CHAPTER SUMMARY

Never stop learning! Being a lifelong learner is essential to your success. Through self-learning, you can gain new skills that will enhance your abilities as a healthcare professional. The internet makes so much information immediately accessible, and much of it is free. Start learning today by listening to a podcast, reading a health blog, or taking an online training course.

RESOURCES

Online Videos—TED Talks

Love, R. "How Nurses Can Help Drive Healthcare Innovation." www.ted.com/talks/rebecca_love_nurse_innovation_saving_ the_future_of_healthcare.

Regis College. "7 TED Talks for Health Care Leaders." https:// online.regiscollege.edu/blog/7-ted-talks-health-care-leaders/.

Online Videos—Agencies

Agency for Healthcare Research and Quality. "TeamSTEPPS Train-ing Videos." www.ahrq.gov/teamstepps/rrs/videos/index.html.

Public Health Emergency. "Hospitals and Health Care Coalitions." www.phe.gov/Preparedness/news/events/NPM18/Pages/ health-care-community.aspx.

Online Journals

American College of Healthcare Executives (ACHE) journals (member log-in required): www.ache.org/learning-center/ publications/journals.

Journal of Medical Internet Research (and all *JMIR* sister journals): www.jmir.org.

Blogs

ACHE blog: http://blog.ache.org.

American Public University System *Emergency & Disaster Management Digest*: https://edmdigest.com.

Centers for Disease Control and Prevention blogs: https://blogs.cdc.gov.

Healthcare Information and Management Systems Society (HIMSS): www.himss.org/news.

Podcasts

Advanced Data Systems Corporation. "15 Healthcare Podcasts You Need to Listen To." www.adsc.com/blog/healthcare-podcasts-you-need-to-listen-to.

HIMSS "Podcasts for Health IT Leaders: Workforce Development." www.himss.org/news/best-podcasts-for-healthcare-it-leaders.

Online Training

FEMA Independent Study Program Courses: https://training.fema.gov/is/crslist.aspx.

US Department of Health and Human Services. "Improving Cultural Competency for Behavioral Health Professionals." https://thinkculturalhealth.hhs.gov/education/behavioral-health.

E-books

Becker Hospital's Review e-books: www.beckershospitalreview.com/multimedia/e-books.html.

Free-eBooks.net: www.free-ebooks.net/health.

National Institute of Neurological Disorders and Stroke e-books: https://catalog.ninds.nih.gov/ninds/term/eBook.

Digital Magazines

ACHE *Healthcare Executive*: https://healthcareexecutive.org.

American Public University System *A Public Health Perspective on the Opioid Crisis—Free Digital Magazine:* https://inpublicsafety.com/2018/11/public-health-perspective-on-the-opioid-crisis/.

Becker's Hospital Review: www.beckershospitalreview.com.

Hands-On Practice

MedSims from WebMD/Medscape: www.medsims.com/medical-simulation-methodology/.

Minerva Medical Simulation Inc.: https://full-code.com.

REFERENCES

Cantrell, J. 2014. "How Did Elon Musk Learn Enough About Rockets to Run SpaceX?" *Forbes*. Published July 16. www.forbes.com/sites/quora/2014/07/16/how-did-elon-musk-learn-enough-about-rockets-to-run-spacex-cofounder-jim-cantrell-answers.

Doughman, A. 2011. "Disney Advises Hospitals and Doctors on Improving Patient Experience." *Orlando Sentinel.* Published July 15. www.orlandosentinel.com/health/os-xpm-2011-07-15-os-disney-hospitals-20110715-story.html.

Martin, G. 2019. "The Meaning and Origin of the Expression: It's Not Rocket Science." Accessed September 12. www.phrases. org.uk/meanings/its-not-rocket-science.html.

CHAPTER 7

Job Prep

THIS CHAPTER FOCUSES on job preparation—key activities you need to accomplish before and during your job search. It also identifies and offers solutions for major obstacles you will encounter in your job search. If you know what employers really want and how they can be expected to behave, then you can better anticipate the job prep that will be required for a successful search. This chapter provides such context.

CHAPTER KEYWORDS

- Resume
- Artificial intelligence
- Applicant tracking system
- Recruiters
- Headhunters
- Job applications
- Bots

JOB PREP IN THE DIGITAL AGE

Preparing for a job search ("job prep") has become especially challenging with the rise of digital technologies and the growing use of artificial intelligence (AI). AI is used increasingly in applicant tracking systems (ATSs) to screen job applications, resumes, and cover letters, as well as to perform other recruitment-related functions. The former CEO of IBM, Ginni Rometty, revealed in a recent interview that the company's human resources (HR) department receives more than 8,000 resumes a day. IBM found that AI makes it possible for HR departments to screen that many resumes without increasing the number of HR staff. In fact, at IBM, implementation of AI allowed the company to reduce the size of its HR department by about 30 percent (Fortt 2019).

So, it is not just about having AI screen your resume; you also likely will interact with fewer humans in HR. As we will discuss in chapter 8, your online interviews may involve AI, too. Figuring out how to get past AI screens and reach a human requires more work (Doyle 2019b). If you do not know how to do this, you will be at a serious disadvantage in your job search.

RESUME OR CV?

Resumes and curricula vitae (CVs) are similar but different, and the terms should not be used interchangeably. The main differences between the two are length and purpose. A CV is a summary record of your education and career history, whereas a resume is usually brief—a one- or two-page listing of your skills and achievements that can be organized as you see fit, updated frequently, and custom-tailored to specific jobs. Resumes are the item most often requested of job applicants (Doyle 2019a).

If resumes are so frequently requested, then why bother using a CV? Resumes, as it happens, are particularly useful when you are applying for entry-level positions. CVs, on the other hand, work well when you have more experience and professional accomplishments. In addition, if you have unconventional education or experience, you may want to use a CV to provide more detail and context (Scott 2014).

Your resume should not include your photo. Although including a photo may be acceptable in some industries, it isn't standard in healthcare. Also, if you want to apply for a federal job, USAJOBS (the federal government's employment site) does not allow certain kinds of personal information, including photos (USAJOBS 2020).

WRITING A RESUME

In today's environment, employers are increasingly using resume screening software, also often referred to as *filters*, *robots*, or *bots*, as a component of their ATS. Thus, the resume you are writing may not be scrutinized by humans, at least not initially. Because you won't know if the hiring organization uses an ATS to screen (and possibly reject) your resume, consider the following:

- Smaller employers—those with fewer than 50 workers— probably won't use software to initially screen resumes. So, if you are applying for a job at a small physician group practice or laboratory facility, you likely will be dealing with humans.
- Midsize and large employers are more likely to use software to screen resumes. Thus, if you are applying for a job in a large hospital, health system, insurance company, or large physician group practice, you could encounter the use of an ATS.

- Fully 70 percent of resumes submitted will be rejected by employers using an ATS (Doyle 2019b).

If you know you are writing a resume for a human, there are basic items and keywords to include, as well as options for formatting. Many books explain how to write a resume, and some offer templates (see the Resources section at the end of this chapter).

Going forward, however, more and more HR departments will likely be using AI to screen and track job applicants because an ATS saves time and money. So, assume you are writing for a robot, and be aware of steps you can take to enhance your chances of getting past the employer's ATS screen (Doyle 2019b).

Getting Past Resume Screens

Knowing how to get your resume successfully past screening software is essential. Here are some tips to assist you (Doyle 2019b; ZipJob 2016):

- Be sure to use keywords that are specific to healthcare. Resources that can help you identify such keywords range from professional associations such as the American College of Healthcare Executives to Monster.com, a popular job search site (see the Resources section at the end of this chapter for additional information).
- Look closely at the job posting, focusing especially on the requested qualifications. Restate these qualifications in your resume.
- Include identifiable skills that healthcare employers generally prefer, both tangible and intangible (again, see the Resources section for more information).

- Use a standard, professional resume format. You can present your resume information in a variety of formats, including reverse chronological (work history with most recent job first), functional (with a focus on skills and experience), or a combination of both. Do your homework here:
  - Consult LinkedIn for advice on formatting.
  - Consult your professional network, such as individuals you met at conferences or other members of the professional associations you belong to.
  - Ask current employees of the organization what format is preferred.
  - Call or e-mail the organization's HR department and directly ask which format is preferred.
  - Avoid fancy designs—fancy can confuse AI filters.
  - Use widely accepted fonts such as Arial, Calibri, or Times New Roman.
  - Unless the employer specifies otherwise, submit Microsoft Word documents—they are most easily processed by screening software.
  - Follow all submission instructions—AI screens are machine based and are reviewing your resume to make sure everything requested is in place.

Because most midsize and large companies are using an ATS to screen applicants, at least initially, the strategy of sending out mass mailings of your resume could be problematic. Instead, customize your resume to each job you're applying for by ensuring that the content of your resume and cover letter match the qualifications contained in the job description (Salpeter 2012). AI screens are searching for specific terms and content associated with the job description and posting. A generic resume won't make it through the screening process.

> ### Action Items
>
> 1. Watch the video "How to Get Your Resume Past Resume Screening Software" (see ZipJob 2016 in References section).
> 2. Revise your resume to get it past ATS screens.

WRITING A COVER LETTER

The cover letter is just as important as the resume. It supplements what is in your resume, going beyond the factual details to add your personality and communicate who you are. A cover letter should make the employer want to hire you, or at least interview you. A cover letter can make you stand out from the crowd of other applicants. So don't make the mistake of thinking that a generic cover letter, such as the following, is acceptable:

Dear Hiring Manager,

Enclosed you will find my resume applying for your open position in the marketing department. Don't hesitate to contact me if you have questions.

Sincerely,
John Doe

Unfortunately, many job applicants spend a lot of time creating the perfect resume, then submit it with a less-than-memorable cover letter that opens with a standard greeting such as "To Whom It May Concern" or "Dear HR." Never do this! If the job posting doesn't supply the name of the hiring manager, do some research to find out who that person likely is. Begin with LinkedIn and visit the employer's website. If you know someone inside the organization, reach out to them for the name to use in addressing the letter. Demonstrate that you have put some effort into your letter.

The best way to organize your cover letter is to match your qualifications with those listed in the job posting. Employers frequently include a laundry list of desired qualifications, many of them preferred. But you can figure out which ones are key. Provide brief summaries of previous experience that reflect those key qualifications.

Cover letters should be brief—preferably no more than one page. If your cover letter is longer than your resume, start over. Remember that if the employer is using software to screen resumes, your cover letter might be read by a robot, too. Some of the strategies described earlier for getting past resume screens apply to cover letters as well, especially those relating to the use of fonts and Microsoft Word documents.

Avoid the following mistakes in your cover letter (Glassdoor 2020):

- Overusing the pronoun *I*
- Offering too much detail
- Using clichés such as *self-starter* or *detail oriented* and overused phrases such as *Please feel free to contact me*
- Including irrelevant information that may distract the reader
- Overstating or falsifying your skills and qualifications
- Forgetting to proofread your letter carefully for typos and grammatical errors

Is a Cover Letter Always Required?

Sometimes you don't need to submit a cover letter. If applying directly for a job on LinkedIn, for example, you often can skip the cover letter:

(continued)

- Use LinkedIn to identify jobs that interest you.

- Attach your resume.

- Click send.

Keep in mind that cover letters are intended to give more information about you. If you don't feel confident letting your resume alone speak for you, include a cover letter that furnishes more information about who you are.

As a general rule, if you fail to get responses after submitting your resume without a cover letter, then it is time to sit down and draft a personalized one.

ONLINE JOB APPLICATIONS

When you submit an online job application, you will probably be asked to include a resume and perhaps a cover letter. Read all instructions carefully. If you forget something, it will be your loss, regardless of whether humans or robots are screening your application. Leaving something out indicates a degree of sloppiness that employers don't want—especially in healthcare, where neglecting the tiniest detail can literally be a matter of life or death. HR departments that use an ATS won't notify you about missing items—your application simply won't make it past the initial screen.

However, the ATS most likely won't discard your application. Instead, applications are typically stored in an online database where they can be retrieved by HR staff for future use. Yes, you may have been screened out for a job now only to find out, months later, that the organization is reconsidering your application. Therefore, make sure your resume and cover letter are error free. Don't include acronyms or other abbreviations—spell everything out, because in healthcare such information is subject to change with new legislation or changes in reimbursement guidelines. Be sure to complete all fields in the online application. Screens and filters can reject you if you don't complete every item. Human HR staff might pass you by, too (Salpeter 2012).

Online Job Application Tips

- Assume an ATS is being used.

- When you apply for a job that interests you, don't bookmark the link—companies regularly pull job postings, and links go dead.

- Instead, save the job posting as a screenshot or a Word or PDF document so that you can track the jobs you've applied for and follow up later.

Source: Ryan (2016).

You can also use your smartphone to submit job applications while on the go. Keeping track of all of your submitted applications on your phone is easy, too, with Google Sheets. Using Google Sheets, you can create a spreadsheet that shows all the jobs you have applied for and the status of each application. You can include notes indicating the contact person, what documents you have sent them and when, and any responses received. To facilitate correspondence, you can also set up a digital signature on your phone. For example, by adding HelloSign to your e-mail account, you can sign documents online with a legally binding e-signature—and thus avoid the need to print, sign, scan, and forward documents to a prospective employer (Kramer 2018).

FOLLOWING UP

In the past, job applicants usually received some type of acknowledgment that their application had been received and information on how the rest of the process would unfold. Today, circumstances vary. Organizations that use an ATS will most likely send a digital acknowledgment, possibly a text message, like the following:

Dear John,

Danbury Hospital has received your application for the position in the billing department. Should you be selected for an interview, we will notify you by June 3. We request that you do not contact us unless you are selected for an interview.

Thank you for your interest in Danbury Hospital.

Sincerely,
June Smith, HR Manager

Small organizations that still rely on human screening may also send an automated response to your online application, but often they will contact you only for an interview. Discarded applications often end up in the "circular file" (wastebasket) without any acknowledgment, especially in smaller organizations that have limited resources.

Should you follow up personally with a card or e-mail message if you don't receive any notice that your application was received? First, check the job posting. If it instructs job applicants not to contact the organization, don't follow up.

If the job posting contains no caveats about contacting the organization, wait a week and then follow up with a phone call, an e-mail, or a letter to the hiring manager if you have or can obtain the relevant contact information. A LinkedIn message may work, too. When following up by e-mail, make sure the subject line includes the position name and specifies that the message is in follow-up to a job application. Among your follow-up questions, ask if the hiring manager has received your application and if any additional information is needed. Also, ask if there is a timeline for the hiring process (Crawford 2019).

EARLY CAREERIST CASE

Contacting the Organization Without Permission

Sidney was wondering what to do. Two weeks earlier, she had submitted a job application to a large health system in the neighboring state, about a seven-hour drive from home. The position was an entry-level one in the admissions office. Sidney had received an automated acknowledgment that her application had been received. The acknowledgment also stated that the organization would be in touch if it decided to schedule an interview.

Even though Sidney had been waiting only two weeks, it seemed more like two months. Why? Sidney really wanted this job. She had done a lot of research on the organization and the city it served. Almost 35 percent of the population spoke Spanish, a language Sidney was fluent in. She had spent a summer doing volunteer work in Costa Rica, and she had also volunteered in the admissions department of a local community hospital. Sidney believed her qualifications made her perfect for the job.

On Monday, she woke up and decided she couldn't wait any longer. She hastily packed a bag and started out on the seven-hour drive to see if she might be able to speak with someone in the health system's HR department. Nine hours later (there was a lot of traffic), Sidney arrived at the facility and asked if she could speak with someone in HR. She was told that was not possible because the entire HR department was attending a retreat for several days. Sidney then asked if she could speak with someone in the admissions department. The answer was that no unscheduled appointments were allowed without prior authorization.

Distraught, Sidney headed for the cafeteria to get some coffee. It was crowded, but there were a few open seats. She

(continued)

sat down at a table after asking if it would be okay to join the others seated there. Within a few minutes, Sidney discovered that at least three of the people at the table worked in admissions. She told them how she had just driven nine hours in hopes of getting a job there. It turned out to be Sidney's lucky day: She was invited to meet with the admissions director. Sidney had planned ahead and brought a copy of her resume with her.

The admissions director approved of Sidney's initiative and also liked what she saw on her resume. All that remained was for Sidney's references to be checked. Of course, everyone said she was a real go-getter who always showed initiative.

Sidney's story is not the norm. She was prepared and took advantage of opportunities. There are stories of other applicants who were turned away when they dropped by unannounced.

USING OUTSIDE RESOURCES

Searching for a job can be overwhelming, especially if you are new to the job market. There is so much to do and so much to learn. How do you avoid making mistakes if you have never searched for a job before? Well, you can use a recruiter. Recruiters don't find you a job; they are hired by employers to fill open positions. This is a significant distinction. Recruiters determine if your skills and experience are a match for job placement. If they aren't, your resume will remain in their database, and you could be contacted in the future if another position opens up for which you are a good match.

Recruiters can make the job search process easier in some respects, and for those who want someone by their side, recruiters not only expedite the process but also offer helpful guidance. They can review your resume and give you advice in the event you get an interview. They have access to a large network of employers and likely will save you time (Cameron 2020).

If you have few skills and limited experience, however, recruiters may not be able to match you with an employer. The reason is that recruiters are paid by employers to fill open positions, not to find you a job.

A special type of recruiter, headhunters, actively look for candidates to fill open positions for employers. Headhunters tend to represent employers seeking to fill higher-paying, senior-level positions for which applicants must be commensurately highly qualified. Headhunters usually charge a fee, which is paid by the employer (Marquit 2020).

A Few Words of Advice

- Some recruiters and headhunters may attempt to charge job seekers a fee (e.g., a percentage of their salary). Be sure to read all agreements or contracts that you sign.

- Avoid paying for such services when you are new in your career.

- Since you will be searching for jobs throughout your lifetime, you may as well just dive in and learn to search on your own. Consider the experience an adventure.

- You can also take a hybrid approach: Search for jobs on your own *and* consult with a recruiter. Whatever works for you!

CHAPTER SUMMARY

This chapter examined key elements of preparing for your job search. Writing a resume and cover letter is an important undertaking, and one that is becoming more challenging with the increased use of AI and ATS screens. Submitting a job application today requires more research and thought on your part than in the past. Searching for a job has never been fun or easy, but once you have successfully landed a job, the next search won't seem so daunting.

One option is to use outside resources, such as recruiters and headhunters. However, if you are new to your career, you may not have the requisite skills and experience to be placed with an employer. Job prep is a lot of work. However, getting a master's degree wasn't easy either. You are used to challenges and hard work and eager to learn new things. Job prep is just one of the steps on your career pathway.

RESOURCES

Amazon Best Sellers for Job Resumes: www.amazon.com/Best-Sellers-Books-Job-Resumes/zgbs/books/2579.

American College of Healthcare Executives. "ACHE Healthcare Executive Competencies Assessment Tool." www.ache.org/-/media/ache/career-resource-center/competencies_booklet.pdf.

Book Authority. "6 Best New CV and Resume Books to Read." https://bookauthority.org/books/new-cv-and-resume-books.

DeCarlo, L. *Resumes for Dummies*, 8th ed. New York: John Wiley & Sons.

Doyle, A. "Top Skills and Attributes Employers Look For." The Balance Careers. www.thebalancecareers.com/top-skills-employers-want-2062481.

Doyle, A. "What Does a Health Care/Hospital Administrator Do?" The Balance Careers. www.thebalancecareers.com/health-care-hospital-administrator-skills-2062403.

Healthcare Administration. "Do You Have What It Takes to Become a Healthcare Administrator?" www.healthcareadministration.com/healthcare-administration-5-core-competencies/.

Monster.com. "Top 5 Skills and Qualifications for Health Services Administration." www.monster.com/career-advice/article/top-5-skills-and-qualifications-for-health-services-administration.

Resume Genius Team. "How to Write a Resume: The Complete Guide." https://resumegenius.com/how-to-write-a-resume.

REFERENCES

Cameron, A. 2020. "7 Reasons to Use a Recruiter to Find a Job." TopResume. Accessed January 16. www.topresume.com/career-advice/7-reasons-to-use-a-recruiter-to-find-a-job.

Crawford, H. 2019. "How to Follow Up on a Job Application." *U.S. News & World Report*. Published June 4. https://money.usnews.com/money/blogs/outside-voices-careers/articles/how-to-follow-up-on-a-job-application.

Doyle, A. 2019a. "The Difference Between a Resume and a Curriculum Vitae." The Balance Careers. Updated July 30. https://thebalancecareers.com/cv-vs-resume-2058495.

———. 2019b. "How to Get Your Resume Past the Applicant Tracking System." The Balance Careers. Updated May 17. https://thebalancecareers.com/how-to-get-your-resume-past-the-applicant-tracking-system-2063135.

Fortt, J. 2019. "IBM's Ginni Rometty: AI Will Change 100 Percent of Jobs." Published April 3. CNBC. www.cnbc.com/video/2019/04/03/ibms-ginni-rometty-ai-will-change-100-percent-of-jobs.html.

Glassdoor. 2020. "How to Write a Cover Letter." Accessed January 16. www.glassdoor.com/blog/guide/how-to-write-a-cover-letter/.

Kramer, J. 2018. "6 Steps That'll Prepare You to Apply to Any Job at Any Time." Glassdoor. Published May 22. www.glassdoor.com/blog/apply-to-any-job-at-any-time/.

Marquit, M. 2020. "Using Headhunters and Career Counselors to Get a Job—Is It Worth It?" MoneyCrashers. Accessed January 16. www.moneycrashers.com/are-job-headhunters-career-counselor-gurus-worth-it/.

Ryan, L. 2016. "How to Outwit an Online Job Application." *Forbes*. Published January 31. www.forbes.com/sites/lizryan/2016/01/31/how-to-outwit-an-online-job-application/.

Salpeter, M. 2012. "The 9 Best Tips for Submitting an Online Job Application." *U.S. News & World Report*. Published July 11. https://money.usnews.com/money/blogs/outside-voices-careers/2012/07/11/the-9-best-tips-for-submitting-an-online-job-application.

Scott, J. 2014. "When Should You Use a CV Instead of a Resume?" Nexxt. Published May 12. www.nexxt.com/articles/when-should-you-use-a-cv-instead-of-a-resume--14819-article.html.

USAJOBS. 2020. "What Should I Leave Out of My Resume?" Accessed January 16. www.usajobs.gov/Help/faq/application/documents/resume/what-to-leave-out/.

ZipJob. 2016. "How to Get Your Resume Past Resume Screening Software." Published September 1. www.youtube.com/watch?v=gxsl-tgM-ZE.

CHAPTER 8

Interviews

THIS CHAPTER EXAMINES the important role of interviewing in your job search. Whether you meet with a prospective employer face-to-face (F2F) or have an online interview, the same key elements—planning in advance, rehearsing, and your appearance—are essential. The only difference is that online interviews are mediated by technology.

Online interviews offer certain advantages—for example, you don't have to travel anywhere, and you are in control of the physical environment in which the interview takes place. However, technology also adds one more item you must pay attention to, and it may increase your stress level because your preparations must include making sure, ahead of time, that the technology works. After all, you don't want to experience connectivity problems during the interview. This chapter explains how to deal with such challenges and also examines the phenomenon of interviewing with artificial intelligence (AI), such as robots, bots, and chatbots.

ADVANCE PLANNING AND PREPARATION

The healthcare environment encompasses a variety of organizations, including small and large physician group practices, local and national health systems, and insurance companies—not to mention pharmacies, diagnostic laboratories, consulting firms, and more. There are also local, state, and federal government entities that employ graduates of health services administration and public health programs. Some organizations are more tech savvy than others, and some jobs won't require you to be highly skilled in the use of technology beyond day-to-day applications such as e-mail. Regardless, you must be prepared for interviewing in the digital environment, unless you want to miss out on future career opportunities.

During an online interview, always remember that you must do everything you can to retain control on your end. In the digital environment, you can easily feel overwhelmed by technology. But don't—the organizational and planning skills described here will help you deliver your absolute best interview performances in the digital environment.

Technology: Make Sure Everything Works

Online job interviews typically take place via webcam, and most laptops today have a webcam built in. The interviewer will specify the video conferencing software to be used, and you should download it ahead of time. Some employers may use a proprietary software program that is unfamiliar to you. Don't panic—with advance planning, you have time to figure it out.

In addition to downloading the specified software ahead of time, test it so that you won't have technical difficulties during the actual interview. Be certain the camera is properly situated so that it shows your entire face and not just one particular side. Test any microphones or headsets. Finally, ensure that all log-in credentials work.

Among the most popular video conferencing tools are the following (We Are Virtual Assistants 2020):

- **Skype** is the video conferencing software with which you are likely most familiar because it is widely used for scheduled events, including interviews. It is free to download, and you can use it anywhere in the world.
- **FaceTime** is for Apple devices, such as the iPhone, iPad, and iPod Touch. It offers both portrait and landscape modes, and if you're using a phone or tablet, the back camera can be used to show the viewer something else in your surroundings. Consider this interview wallpaper, because it's what the interviewer will see in the background during your video call.
- **Google Hangouts** works on all computers, and apps for both Apple and Android devices enable you to connect with everyone. The only requirement is that you have a Google account. Hangouts can be accessed from within your Gmail or when you're using Google Chat (and soon, these apps will be replaced by Hangouts Chat and Hangouts Meet). You can invite friends to participate in your interview test runs and even record them for later critique.

Environment: Eliminate Noise, Clutter, and Distractions

In a digital interview, you're the one who has control over the environment. Here are some tips to optimize it:

- Select a quiet location with good lighting. If natural lighting is available, open the blinds. If lighting is a problem, place a table or desk lamp on each side of the screen.
- Lock down the location for both practice sessions and the actual interview. Make sure that everyone who shares your residence or office space stays away for a specified period. Send them an e-mail and text message on the day of the actual interview as a reminder.
- Post a note on the door of the room being used for the interview, advising people not to bother you or even knock.
- Put pets in another room, or ask a friend to take them for an hour or so.
- Declutter your interview space, including what is visible behind you, to avoid distracting the interviewer. A blank wall is best—take down posters, memorabilia, and even diplomas because reflections from the glass in picture frames can be distracting.
- Have a pen and paper within easy reach so you can take notes.
- Have a copy of your resume at hand in case you need to refer to it for detailed information on past jobs, job titles, and dates of employment. You don't want to scramble for your resume mid-interview.
- Use a chair that doesn't move or swivel, as this could lead to unnecessary movements that may distract and be misinterpreted by the interviewer as nervousness. Your aim is to appear confident.
- Make sure you are at eye level with the camera.

- Use headphones to reduce any background noise or reverberation from your computer's audio speakers.
- Find an optimal place to post any reminders to yourself— for example, on the side of your computer screen. Just make sure you don't have to look down to view them.

Smartphone Interviews

If you must use your smartphone for an interview, make sure that you have prepared, planned, and practiced appropriately. Follow all instructions and suggestions shared so far, but pay special attention to the following, too:

- Don't interview in a noisy, public place such as a coffee shop or sitting on a bench in a park with people walking and cycling past you.
- Never attempt to interview while driving.
- Never conduct a phone interview in a restroom. Some people have done so and learned, to their detriment, that restrooms are not private, noise-free places.
- Stabilize your phone by using a holder.
- Make sure your phone is at eye level so that you are not seen as looking down at it.
- Make sure your phone is fully charged. Disable any alarms, and use the "do not disturb" setting to silence notifications and call rings.

APPEARANCE: DRESS FOR THE JOB YOU WANT

How you present yourself in an interview is critically important, even if the interview is taking place online or via video. Don't make the mistake of feeling too comfortable and dressing casually because you are at home. Your interviewers will most likely be in an office setting and expect professional attire and grooming from any job candidate, whether interviewed F2F or remotely.

Follow these tips:

- Even though you will likely be seen only from the waist up, dress professionally from head to toe, just in case you stand up at some point.
- To determine which colors work best, let your practice runs decide. Bold colors may flatter you in a F2F interview but appear distracting online. Over the internet, some colors can even hurt the interviewer's eyes.
- Check out what newscasters or people being interviewed on TV are wearing. Although prints and even some solid colors were once no-no's, they may be acceptable now because of advances in technology.
- Do not wear noisy jewelry or long, dangling earrings. Also skip the bracelets that indicate your hobbies or interests. Once you're hired, you can share your personal side. The interview is all about being professional.
- Avoid wearing clothing that may be distracting, such as frills or multiple layers.
- Make sure your hair is not a distraction. Hair should be pulled back and off your face. Avoid playing with or rearranging your hair during the interview.
- Find out ahead of time what the prospective employer's policy is on tattoos and facial hair, such as beards. The healthcare field tends to be conservative, especially if you are interacting directly with patients. You can't rely totally on what those who already work at the organization tell you because what is acceptable in the business office may not be permitted in clinical areas. Organizational policies vary, and you may be asked to cover up your tattoos while at work.

INTERVIEW QUESTIONS: ENSURING YOUR BEST PERFORMANCE

Much as you might prepare for an exam, you should anticipate possible interview questions and craft answers ahead of time. Ideally, your responses will be brief and specific to the job posting. Questions commonly asked in online interviews include the following (Lee 2017):

- "Who are you and why should we hire you?" This question lets you talk about yourself, but make sure you use terms and phrases in the job description. Talk about your accomplishments.

- "How did you learn of this job opening?" This one is easy to answer. Just be honest and don't fabricate an answer to impress the interviewer. If you heard about the job opening in an elevator, tell them so.

- "What do you know about this organization?" Responding to this question requires some advance research on your part. View the employer's website. Check them out on LinkedIn, Indeed, or Glassdoor. Don't try to bluff your way through this one, as it will only show you are unprepared and dishonest.

- "Are you currently employed? If so, why do you want to change jobs?" Be as honest as possible here, but in some instances you should not reveal everything. For example, your current employer may be experiencing financial problems but wishes to keep this information private. So, give your response to this question a great deal of thought, and run it by your mentors.

- "What are your strengths and weaknesses?" Never say your weakness is that you are too dedicated or work too hard. Such answers are cliché. You can respond by identifying a skill that you are working to improve. For example:

"I recognize that I need to be more culturally competent to understand the demographic makeup of my community, so I've begun taking courses in Spanish."

- "What are your salary expectations?" Explore websites such as Glassdoor to find pay scales for similar positions. Prepare thoroughly for this question. You would do well to quote a slightly higher salary than what the employer is willing to pay, as it will permit flexibility in negotiating should you make it to that point in the process.

The primary goal of the interview is to successfully move on to the next step in the process, which may be a job offer. Additional tips to help you reach this goal include the following (Koenig 2017):

- Do not be rude or arrogant toward the interviewer.
- Displaying confidence is fine, but don't appear to be full of yourself.
- Don't ask obvious questions. They are time wasters.
- Never disparage anyone, especially current or past employers.
- Don't share too much personal information about yourself.
- Don't be the first one to bring up the compensation package.
- Never lie during the interview. Lies are hard to remember. They are also tough to walk back if subsequently uncovered during the interview.
- Don't get upset if interviewers confuse you with another applicant. They can't possibly remember all of the details from your application, and they are likely interviewing several candidates on the same day. Remain professional and remind them of your accomplishments.

- Don't try to control the interview by dominating the conversation.
- Don't forget to ask questions when the interview is concluding. The interviewer will likely ask if you have any questions, so make a list ahead of time. For example, you could ask questions related to what the employer will expect of you if you are hired:
  - "What do you expect me to contribute in this role during the first three months?"
  - "What do you anticipate being the major accomplishments of this role in the first six months?"
  - "What are the challenges that this role will experience during the first year?"
- If you make a mistake, have a recovery strategy:
  - Take a breath and admit the error.
  - Remain confident and address the mistake with a positive comment. For example: "I'm not very familiar with that strategy, but I have some ideas about working with it."

PRACTICE, PRACTICE, PRACTICE!

Based on what you've read here, create a checklist of items to prepare for, including technology, environment, and appearance. You can use this list when you conduct interview test runs with trusted friends or mentors. In addition:

- Be punctual—that is, online and ready five to ten minutes before the interview is scheduled to start. Even if it's just a test run, you want to respect the time of the friend or mentor who is helping you.
- Use Google Hangouts to share video recordings of practice sessions with selected friends for review and evaluation.

- If anything goes wrong during the test run, fix it. Do another one and make sure all is good.
- Get input from others. Friends and mentors can bring different perspectives and spot things that you might miss.
- Scrutinize your practice sessions carefully. Make sure that what you're wearing looks professional and that your hair is in place. Is your demeanor appropriate—do you appear confident and enthusiastic, rather than nervous?
- Practice sitting with excellent posture and keep your head up.
- Ensure you make good eye contact. Making eye contact isn't natural, so practice it.
- Be sure to look straight at the camera, not at the small image of yourself in the corner. Again, this takes practice.
- Don't post any practice sessions on social media.

Action Items

1. Watch the following videos on YouTube:
   - "How to Prepare for Video Interviews" (see Work It Daily 2018 in References section)
   - "How to Prepare for an Online Skype Job Interview in 2019" (see Clark 2018 in References section)
2. From each video, identify three items that you learned that will be helpful.
3. Practice your interviewing skills using the following online resources:
   - American College of Healthcare Executives (ACHE) Interview Prep Tool: www.ache.org/ career-resource-center/build-your-personal-brand/ interview-prep-tool
   - My Interview Simulator—Online Edition: http:// myinterviewsimulator.com

WHAT TO WATCH FOR AND DO DURING AI INTERVIEWS

The cost of hiring an employee is high, with a price tag estimated to be upwards of $3,500. Some employers reduce this cost by using AI software that simulates conversation with human users. The first-round "interview" may take place on the employer's website and consist of chatting with the job applicant, setting up an interview appointment, and asking if the applicant has any questions about the hiring process. Increasingly, applicants are encountering nonhumans in the recruitment process, whether they are aware of it or not (Headley 2019; Phillips 2019).

During an interview using AI, the software records and analyzes your speech and visual cues. An algorithm determines if you are a good fit for the job opening based on your answers to interview questions and your level of enthusiasm about the job's duties and responsibilities (Bauman 2018).

Even though AI is mostly used in the retail industry, during the past decade much of healthcare has been influenced by retail, and the need to reduce costs is a major ongoing challenge. If you find yourself being interviewed by some type of AI (e.g., a bot, chatbot, video screen with a humanoid, or telephone call with an automated voice), take it seriously if you want to move on to the next step and reach human scrutiny. Tips for interviewing with AI include the following (Lopaze 2020):

- Don't try to engage or develop rapport with the interviewer—they are not human!
- Don't turn on the charm. Be polite and professional.
- Don't depend on your charisma. It won't register with the software.
- Don't give vague answers.
- Do focus on the job posting, and use words and phrases derived from it because they are what the software is looking for.

- Do speak clearly and precisely, and answer the question that was asked.
- Do remember that visual cues are important. So, watch your body language, including posture and eye contact.
- Do take control of your facial expressions. Bots can detect microexpressions (involuntary emotional reactions) that often go undetected by human interviewers.

FOLLOWING UP: THANK-YOU NOTES

Are traditional thank-you notes after an interview still relevant? Absolutely! Although it adds another item to your list of things to do when searching for a job, such follow-up can make all the difference (Lorenz 2018). Most recruiters and managers expect a thank-you note from interviewees, and receiving one can affect the decision-making process (Luckwaldt 2017). One Career-Builder survey found that 57 percent of job applicants don't send a thank-you note, even though not sending a thank-you note is one of five job-search mistakes that can keep you from getting hired (Kofler 2019).

Thank-you notes have the potential to shift the balance in your favor, especially when you are competing for the job with other applicants of similar backgrounds, qualifications, and skills. But any follow-up has challenges. It must be prompt, thoughtful, and something other than a perfunctory one-line e-mail, which actually could negatively affect your application. If you have time to write only one line, just skip it.

You can also use a follow-up thank-you note to clarify any misstatements made during the interview. For example: "I thought about how I described my last job, and I think I need to clarify some of my duties and responsibilities to make sure I present a completely accurate picture." You can also address anything that went wrong during the interview by turning it into a positive. However, be careful here, as it is often best not to remind people about what went wrong, especially if they have already forgotten it. If you cannot turn the situation into a positive, leave it alone (McCord 2020).

What does a follow-up note say about you as a job applicant? It demonstrates that you are courteous and respectful and that you are willing to go beyond what is required. Because so few applicants today follow up by thanking those who took the time to meet with them, you will automatically stand out. Finally, a follow-up note demonstrates your communication skills in written form. And if you send your thank-you e-mail the same day as the interview, you'll gain an advantage over equally qualified candidates (Vogt 2020).

Thus, taking a few minutes to compose a thoughtful follow-up note thanking those who interviewed you is a worthwhile use of your time during a job search. Remember to send the thank-you within 24 hours, personalize the message, and proofread it carefully (Luckwaldt 2017).

CHAPTER SUMMARY

This chapter explored how to successfully manage an interview in the digital environment. Interviewing remotely saves you travel time and may reduce some anxiety because you have control over your environment. However, it also requires more preparation, including making sure the technology works, your environment is optimized, and you appear well on camera. This chapter also examined interview questions and advised what to do if you are interviewed by a bot.

Regardless of how your interview goes—whether you nailed it or could have done better—don't post anything about it on social media. Doing so will discourage employers from inviting you for future interviews. However, do be sure to follow up by sending a thank-you note. It makes a difference!

RESOURCES

ACHE Interview Prep Tool: /www.ache.org/career-resource-center/
build-your-personal-brand/interview-prep-tool.

FaceTime: https://support.apple.com/en-gb/HT204380.

Google Hangouts: https://hangouts.google.com.

My Interview Simulator—Online Edition: http://myinterviewsimulator.
com.

Skype: www.skype.com.

REFERENCES

Bauman, A. 2018. "More People Are Interviewing for Jobs with
'Chatbots.'" CBS New York. Published September 26.
https://newyork.cbslocal.com/2018/09/26/chatbots-
are-replacing-people-in-job-interviews/.

Clark, D. 2018. "How to Prepare for an Online Skype Job Interview
in 2019." YouTube. Posted November 12. www.youtube.com/
watch?v=wBbzI0_HPuM.

Headley, C. W. 2019. "Robots Could Be Conducting Your
Job Interviews by 2020." Ladders. Published March 15. www.
theladders.com/career-advice/robots-could-be-conducting-
your-job-interviews-by-2020.

Koenig, R. 2017. "Job Interview Mistakes to Avoid." *U.S. News &
World Report*. Published November 3. https://money.usnews.
com/money/careers/interviewing/articles/job-interview-
mistakes-to-avoid.

Kofler, S. 2019. "These 5 Simple Mistakes Could Be Costing
You the Job." CareerBuilder. Published June 10.

www.careerbuilder.com/advice/these-5-simple-mistakes-could-be-costing-you-the-job.

Lee, C. 2017. "7 Common Online Interview Questions and Suggested Answers." ezTalks. Published January 18. www.eztalks.com/online-interview/7-common-online-interview-questions-and-suggested-answers.html.

Lopaze, K. 2020. "How to Prepare for a Job Interview When the Interviewer Is a Robot." Job Network. Accessed January 21. www.thejobnetwork.com/how-to-prepare-for-a-job-interview-when-the-interviewer-is-a-robot/.

Lorenz, M. 2018. "Are Post-Interview Thank-You Notes Still a Thing?" CareerBuilder. Published August 19. www.careerbuilder.com/advice/are-postinterview-thankyou-notes-still-a-thing.

Luckwaldt, J. H. 2017. "Hiring Managers to Job Seekers: No Thank-You Note, No Job." CNBC Make It. Published December 19. www.cnbc.com/2017/12/19/hiring-managers-to-job-seekers-no-thank-you-note-no-job.html.

McCord, S. 2020. "3 Times Your Thank You Note Could Make the Difference in Whether or Not You Get the Job." Daily Muse. Accessed January 21. www.themuse.com/advice/3-times-your-thank-you-note-could-make-the-difference-in-whether-or-not-you-get-the-job.

Phillips, A. 2019. "Are Chatbots the Future of Job Recruitment?" Medium. Published April 5. https://chatbotslife.com/are-chatbots-the-future-of-job-recruitment-4ca53a2f1d57.

Vogt, P. 2020. "The Benefits of a Thank You Note After a Job Interview." Monster. Accessed January 21. www.monster.com/career-advice/article/power-of-a-simple-thank-you-note.

We Are Virtual Assistants. 2020. "5 Video Tools to Hold Meetings with Your Clients." Accessed January 21. https://wearevirtualassistants.com/5-video-tools-to-hold-meetings-with-your-clients/.

Work It Daily. 2018. "How to Prepare for Video Interviews." YouTube. Posted January 11. www.youtube.com/watch?v=aevCwBCYWtY.

CHAPTER 9

Digital Networking

"NETWORK! NETWORK! NETWORK!" You hear it constantly from your teachers and colleagues, but what does it mean? And how exactly do you do it?

Networking is about making meaningful relationships. You do this regularly in your personal life without even thinking about it: You make new friends, go to parties and movies with friends and relatives, and maybe even find a love interest. By engaging in such activities, you are developing your personal network. Building your professional network is also very important, particularly early in your career.

CHAPTER KEYWORDS

- Network

- Social media

- Connections

NETWORKING WITH INTENT

One of the best pieces of advice you will ever receive in your life, both personal and professional, is to *live with intent* (Chopra 2015). When you live with intent, you prioritize your time and efforts to focus on the things that really matter to you. Living with intent helps tune out the chaos and background noise that steal your time and energy.

You have probably heard of the theory of six degrees of separation—the idea that everyone on earth is no more than six social connections away from each other. With Facebook, everyone may now be only four social introductions away from everyone else (Daraghmi and Yuan 2014). If we all are already so interconnected, what's the purpose of networking and why should we do it? Well, there is no intent in this sort of connectedness. In healthcare, you must network with intent. *Intentionally* speak to people, *intentionally* learn from others, and *intentionally* build relationships. Doing so will create future opportunities and more connections within one or two degrees of separation. And it just may lead to the perfect collaboration that saves future lives with a health breakthrough!

You need to network with many people. Often, people think that meeting the CEO is going to catapult them to the top. In fact, for most, getting to the top means climbing from the bottom. If you make it to the top by climbing from the bottom, then you will appreciate the hard work and dedication that is needed to get there. During your journey, you will meet others and develop a robust network to support you when you need it.

It's great to network with top leaders, so do aim to include CEOs, vice presidents, and other senior leaders in your networking strategy and activities (you may even find a mentor among them). But network with other health professionals, too—health educators, patient transporters, medical assistants, health unit clerks, supervisors, managers, and anyone else you meet in your career.

> Lou Adler, CEO of Performance-based Hiring Learning Systems and designated LinkedIn influencer, has reported that 85 percent of survey respondents identified networking as their primary means for finding a job (Adler 2016).

NETWORKING IN THE DIGITAL ENVIRONMENT

People commonly think of networking as happening only through face-to-face (F2F) interactions. But in fact, we interact and communicate daily through digital means such as e-mails, texts, video conferences, webinars, social media, and instant messaging. More and more people have jobs that allow them to work remotely from home, and students can now complete their education entirely online. So why not network in the digital environment, too?

LinkedIn

To network in the digital environment, the first thing you must do is create a LinkedIn account. LinkedIn is the social networking site for professionals and businesses. It is like Facebook in that you can connect, post, like, share, and send messages, but it is intended for professional use.

One benefit of LinkedIn is that you can use it to connect with colleagues and other work professionals without sharing your personal activities with them. Thanks to LinkedIn, you don't need to feel obligated to accept work-related requests or invitations on personal social networking sites such as Facebook.

Once you have a LinkedIn account, you can build and optimize your profile to achieve "All-Star" status. LinkedIn has five levels of profiles: Beginner, Intermediate, Advanced, Expert, and All-Star. LinkedIn users with a complete profile are 40 times more likely to receive job opportunities (Libo-on 2016). To reach All-Star status, you need to complete seven areas (McDonald 2015):

1. Profile picture
2. Experience
3. Skills
4. Summary
5. Industry and location
6. Education
7. Connections

LinkedIn suggests five additional steps you can take to improve your profile in mere minutes (see the Resources section at the end of this chapter). These steps can be done on your smartphone using the LinkedIn mobile app.

E-mail

E-mail is a common form of communication, especially in business. You often communicate with your colleagues via e-mail, but did you know you can also use e-mail to network? Building professional relationships is possible via e-mail. When you meet colleagues for the first time—at a work meeting or annual conference, for example—you can follow up with an e-mail expressing your appreciation for their contributions and letting them know you're glad you met them. This sort of interaction is welcoming and may stimulate additional collaboration.

Social Media

Organizations and businesses tend to use social media primarily for marketing and promotion, but healthcare organizations also use it for community outreach. You can engage with other professionals and health agencies using social media.

One survey found that 68 percent of US adults use Facebook, and 35 percent use Instagram (Pew Research Center 2018).

Are there any healthcare organizations that interest you? Or a healthcare leader who inspires you? Start engaging with them on social media. If you are interested in mental health topics, then you can "like" the Substance Abuse and Mental Health Services Administration's Facebook page (see this chapter's Resources section for the URL). If you want to work in emergency management, then follow your local emergency operations center on Twitter. You can learn so much about the work and initiatives of healthcare organizations by interacting with them on social media.

Conferences

Although you can attend some conferences virtually, most conferences are F2F events. You can learn, network, and share your projects at conferences. But when the conferences are over, you should take these in-person experiences and convert them into digital networking opportunities.

- **Meeting people:** At conferences, you will meet many people while walking from your hotel, attending sessions, or having lunch. Take note of their name badges, or ask for their business cards. Request a LinkedIn connection with everyone you meet within 48 hours, and ideally within 24 hours. When you send the invitation, you can include a message stating what a pleasure it was meeting them and highlighting a part of your conversation.

- **Meeting presenters:** When you attend a presentation, you may not have an opportunity to talk to the presenter. It will depend on how many people stay afterward to talk or ask questions, as well as how much time you have until your next session. Regardless, you should always connect with presenters on LinkedIn. If you have questions or would like to send a personalized message, you can also e-mail the presenter.

- **Being a presenter:** When you give a presentation, you will have an audience that is interested in your topic. This is the perfect opportunity to network. Some audience members may approach you afterward to speak with you, but you should try to engage with all of them. At the end of your presentation, ask the attendees to connect with you on LinkedIn or to leave their business cards (you can have a container near the door to collect them). Depending on the size of your audience, you can send each of them a message via LinkedIn or e-mail, thanking them for attending your presentation.

- **Social mixers:** At conferences, there are often social mixers. These provide a more relaxed environment to meet people. Some conferences, such as the annual meeting of the American Public Health Association and the annual Congress on Healthcare Leadership of the American College of Healthcare Executives, offer various university alumni mixers. These events are a great way to engage with fellow alumni and consider future collaborations. At every social mixer, you should ask people about their work and current projects or research interests. Afterward, be sure to connect with them on LinkedIn.

Although LinkedIn is a great tool for professional networking, not all professionals have a LinkedIn account or actively use their LinkedIn account. You will need to tailor your networking efforts according to a person's usage. For example, if you send a request to connect via LinkedIn but the person doesn't accept or respond within two weeks, you may want to follow up by e-mail.

Other F2F Events

Every in-person meeting—whether a classroom training course, local community event, or simple conversation—is an opportunity for you to meet people and expand your network, both physically and digitally. You may meet an influential healthcare leader while getting your oil changed or standing in line at the movies. Be open to conversation, and always be polite and respectful. When you meet someone in healthcare, follow up by sending an invitation to connect on LinkedIn.

Action Items

1. Create a LinkedIn account and build your profile.
2. Connect with at least five health professionals on LinkedIn.
3. Follow a health leader on Twitter.
4. "Like" a healthcare organization's Facebook page.
5. Follow a health cause on Instagram.

CHAPTER SUMMARY

Networking is important in your career, and networking with intent will help you build meaningful relationships. With our tech-busy lives, networking has expanded to the internet, especially with the rise of social media. Having a professional online presence is necessary to seize networking opportunities in the digital environment.

RESOURCES

Fisher, C. "5 Steps to Improve Your LinkedIn Profile in Minutes." https://blog.linkedin.com/2016/08/03/5-steps-to-improve-your-linkedin-profile-in-minutes-.

Leisure Jobs. "The Ultimate LinkedIn Cheat Sheet." www.leisurejobs.com/staticpages/18285/the-ultimate-linkedin-cheat-sheet/.

Substance Abuse and Mental Health Services Administration Facebook page: www.facebook.com/samhsa/.

REFERENCES

Adler, L. 2016. "New Survey Reveals 85% of All Jobs Are Filled via Networking." LinkedIn. Published February 29. www.linkedin.com/pulse/new-survey-reveals-85-all-jobs-filled-via-networking-lou-adler.

Chopra, M. 2015. *Living with Intent: My Somewhat Messy Journey to Purpose, Peace, and Joy.* New York: Harmony Books.

Daraghmi, E. Y., and S.-M. Yuan. 2014. "We Are So Close, Less Than 4 Degrees Separating You and Me!" *Computers in Human Behavior* 30: 273–85.

Libo-on, A. 2016. "The Ultimate LinkedIn Profile Cheat Sheet [Infographic]." *Search Engine Journal.* Published March 16. www.searchenginejournal.com/ultimate-linkedin-profile-cheat-sheet-infographic/.

McDonald, L. 2015. "LinkedIn All-Star Status Rocks & How to Reach It in 7 Steps." LinkedIn. Published December 16. www.linkedin.com/pulse/linkedin-all-star-status-rocks-how-reach-7-steps-lisa-k-mcdonald.

Pew Research Center. 2018. "Social Media Use in 2018." Published March. http://assets.pewresearch.org/wp-content/uploads/sites/14/2018/03/01105133/PI_2018.03.01_Social-Media_FINAL.pdf.

CHAPTER 10

Self-Evaluation

EVALUATION IS THE "determination of the value, nature, character, or quality of something or someone" (Merriam-Webster 2019). Evaluation is an ongoing process. You continually have to know if something is working well and what needs to be improved. This applies to evaluating yourself, too. You should never live in the status quo. You should constantly learn, grow, and improve—both as a person and as a health professional.

CHAPTER KEYWORDS

- Self-evaluation
- Google search
- Continuous improvement

WHAT YOU'VE LEARNED SO FAR

You have learned so much about yourself up to this point. You have taken self-assessments, enhanced your LinkedIn profile, cleaned up your social media activity, developed your digital brand, determined your career plan and goals, and begun networking with other health professionals. Here's a recap of what you've learned in each chapter so far:

1. **Google You:** When you searched for your name and relevant keywords in online search engines, you learned what is discoverable online about you. You found photos of yourself and information about you that is available to anyone on the internet, including employers.

2. **Self-Discovery:** You created your career goals and took self-assessments. You determined if your online persona aligns with your healthcare career goals. Self-discovery is understanding your strengths and abilities in your healthcare career.

3. **Digital Self-Perception:** Digital self-perception is how you see yourself in the online environment. Being aware of who you are and how your values and capabilities contribute to your online persona is essential. Digital self-perception requires that you be honest with yourself.

4. **Digital Self-Branding:** Digital branding is essentially a form of marketing. Your digital brand should differentiate you from other job candidates. The focus is on portraying a consistent image that reflects both tangible and intangible factors.

5. **Self-Determined Career:** *You* are the major influencer of your career. You can be assertive and proactive in obtaining the job roles you want. You created a three-year career plan and established career goals to actively achieve that plan. Since some events outside of your control can affect your planned timeline and future choices, you should reevaluate your goals every year.

6. **Self-Learning:** Learning should not stop after you graduate. Being a lifelong learner is critical to your success. You should self-evaluate your skills frequently and identify how you can improve them. To advance your career, learning new job skills should be your top priority. Many digital resources are available to help you develop new job skills, including online videos, online articles and blogs, podcasts, online training, and e-books and digital magazines.

7. **Job Prep:** Preparing for a job search has become especially challenging with the rise of digital technologies and the growing use of artificial intelligence. Most of your job applications and resumes will be submitted online, so mastering the digital process is important.

8. **Interviews:** You must be prepared for interviewing in the digital environment. Online, video, and phone interviews are becoming increasingly common in the candidate selection process. Being familiar with Skype, FaceTime, and Google Hangouts will help you succeed in online interviews. Understanding the impact of such factors as your background and the attire you select is also important.

9. **Digital Networking:** Networking is about making meaningful relationships. Building your professional network is very important, particularly early in your career. Network with intent—*intentionally* speak to people, *intentionally* learn from others, and *intentionally* build relationships. LinkedIn, social networking sites, and e-mail are all tools you can use to network in the digital environment.

All of these efforts are helping you to leave a positive and professional footprint on your digital path to your healthcare career.

GOOGLE YOU AGAIN

Now that you've made improvements to your online persona and digital footprint, try Googling yourself again. Using chapter 1 as a guide, repeat the searches you did at the beginning of this book.

When you search for yourself online, consider the following:

- Has anything changed since your first search?
- What has improved?
- Does your LinkedIn profile appear in the search results?
- Does the search reveal any new images or content?
- Is there anything you still need to fix?

SELF-EVALUATION

Considering everything you've learned about yourself on this digital journey, how would you evaluate yourself if you were a hiring manager looking at *you* as a job candidate? Evaluating yourself can be hard, especially in an unbiased way. Sometimes we are too hard on ourselves; at other times, we aren't hard enough.

Self-evaluation isn't about picking out all your faults and weaknesses. It's really about understanding your strengths and limitations. You can always continue to build your skill set and knowledge, but you have to regularly check in on how you are doing. Think about the career plan and map you developed in chapter 5. Have you completed any objectives or achieved any goals?

Planning and implementation are both important in health programs, but evaluation is equally important. Similarly, self-evaluation is your opportunity to see how your goals and objectives are measuring up to your career plan (and implementation).

CONTINUE TO IMPROVE

Improvement is a continuous cycle. You never stop learning, growing, or building your skills to improve your abilities as a healthcare professional. You can be a successful leader and still have the potential to become even better.

This book isn't intended to be used only once. You can use the chapters and their activities throughout your healthcare career. Some information will need updating because technology changes rapidly, but you can continue self-learning, taking self-assessments, making three-year career plans, and evaluating your online persona.

Keep asking yourself the following questions on your digital path to your healthcare career:

- What goals do you want to accomplish?
- How can you accomplish those goals?
- How can you improve your skills?
- What do you need to improve to get to your next dream?
- What can you do in the next 12 months to achieve your goals?

As explained in earlier chapters, you should do two things regularly: (1) Evaluate your resume and (2) review job postings. You should evaluate your resume often because your resume is your professional snapshot. Are you missing any skills or knowledge that you need for the job you want or for your next promotion? Continue volunteering, working, and learning to gain those skills and knowledge.

Reviewing job postings regularly will keep you updated about hiring trends, needed credentials, and any changes in the requirements for various healthcare roles. Find out what skills you need, learn those new skills, update your resume, and repeat! Improvement is a continuous cycle. Never quit learning or becoming the best version of you that you can be.

CHAPTER SUMMARY

Self-evaluation is an ongoing process, so reviewing your skills regularly will improve your abilities as a health professional. You have learned so much about yourself—both the online and offline versions. This book will continue to serve as your guide on your digital path as you advance in your healthcare career.

RESOURCE

Moz. "How Search Engines Work: Crawling, Indexing, and Ranking." Chapter 2 in *The Beginner's Guide to SEO*. https://moz.com/beginners-guide-to-seo/how-search-engines-operate.

REFERENCE

Merriam-Webster. 2019. "Evaluation." Accessed August 10. www.merriam-webster.com/dictionary/evaluation.

CHAPTER 11

Social Media Tips

Technology has become embedded in our daily activities—especially social networking sites such as Facebook and Instagram. Connecting with your friends and family on social media can be fun and exciting, but you have to be careful about what you post on the internet.

"A picture is worth a thousand words" is a common saying that originated with a 1921 article by Frederick Barnard, national advertising manager for the Street Railways Advertising Company, titled "One Look Is Worth a Thousand Words." With the rise of the internet, "a thousand words" is an understatement. Given the viral potential of an online photo, a picture could be worth *millions* of words depending on the reactions and comments it gets. A viral photo or video can even be featured in the news or on television because of the response it has received on the internet.

Unfortunately, it is all too easy for posts, images, and videos to be misinterpreted. Consider how often celebrities and politicians have had to apologize for their social media posts or online activities. You want to avoid posting any content that may be considered controversial, because employers and those in your professional network may see it. This chapter explains how to maintain a certain measure of privacy and how to ensure your social media activities stay squeaky clean.

MAKE YOUR PERSONAL SOCIAL MEDIA ACCOUNTS PRIVATE

There are two main reasons you should make your personal social media accounts private. First, people often reveal information on social media that can be used by criminals and others with bad intentions. Second, only your friends and family need to see your personal activities. Before the advent of social media, you could enjoy your weekends without mixing business and pleasure. Now everything you do on your own time may be exposed at work. Keeping your accounts private will help separate your work life from your personal life.

Although each social networking site has different privacy settings (see the Resources section at the end of this chapter), they all share some similarities. First, as the default setting, make sure only your friends or followers can see your posts. If you want to post something publicly, you can always change the setting on the individual post or image. Second, make sure your privacy settings require your approval before any posts or photos in which you are tagged are posted to your timeline or social media account. This will ensure that you see the content and agree to it before it is posted on your social media profile or page.

Any social media account that you use for business can be made public if you so choose. Having both personal and business social media accounts is recommended except in the case of LinkedIn, which should be used only for professional purposes. For example, you can have a Facebook page for business use but still have your personal Facebook account to engage with your friends and family. Keeping your business and personal accounts separate will also help with your self-branding (see chapter 4), especially if you use the same social media handle for all your business accounts.

CLEAN UP YOUR SOCIAL MEDIA CONTENT

Now that you have made your personal accounts private, you need to clean up your social media profiles. Did you know that anyone with access to your page or timeline can copy your post or image—for example, by taking a screenshot—and share it with whomever they want? Just because your account is private doesn't mean your social media content is private. For this reason, the connections you make on social media matter, and they should be limited to people you know.

Here are some tips for reviewing and cleaning up your social media content:

- Remove all inappropriate pictures (e.g., photos of drinking, "flipping the bird," smoking cigarettes, using drugs, acts of violence).
- Delete posts that criticize someone, use sexist or crude humor, contain intentional lies, or could be considered racist or discriminatory (e.g., based on age, disability, genetic information, national origin, pregnancy, religion, race, sex).
- "Unlike" any posts or images that portray discriminatory activities, drug use, terrorism, hate crimes, or prostitution; that use language bashing an individual or organization; or anything else that could be interpreted negatively.

- Bear in mind that whom you follow may not have as much of an impact as what you post, but you still want to exercise caution in following others. For example, you don't want to follow a person or group that is known to be involved in illegal activity. If you do, you could be perceived as supporting this behavior.
- Check all of your social media accounts—Facebook, Twitter, Instagram, Pinterest, Snapchat, YouTube, LinkedIn, and any others you use.
- Don't share your deepest thoughts and personal feelings on social media for the world to see. Facebook is not a journal. Instead, keep your posts superficial and your comments light, as you would in a conversation in a coffee shop or at a business social mixer.

THINK BEFORE YOU POST OR LIKE

We are fortunate to live in a free country and enjoy freedom of speech, but it's best to refrain from polarized topics on social media. This doesn't mean that you can't support causes you care about or that you have to quit working toward social change. Rather, it's about being considerate and civil toward others who don't think like you or who may disagree with your views.

It's okay to think and act differently than others do. Diversity should be embraced. But it's also acceptable to "agree to disagree." In fact, you will face such situations in the workplace.

Respect should always be the foundation of your communications, whether they are verbal or written and whether they take place in the physical or digital environment. Being behind a computer, tablet, or smartphone screen doesn't give you (or anyone) permission to be disrespectful toward others.

Even though you may keep your social media accounts private, you should post as if the world can see it. Would you want your parents, kids, or employer seeing that photo or comment? If the answer is no, then don't post it! Remember, even if you delete something you posted, someone may already have taken a screenshot of it.

But it's not just about *what* you post. It's also about what you "like" on social media or online sites such as YouTube. If you like something, people may think you agree with or support the post or the activity it portrays, even it is just a joke or meme.

Many people post vulgar and inappropriate things online, but they may work in industries where their career won't be affected by such posts. In healthcare, we serve people from multiple backgrounds and cultures, so diversity and inclusion are vital. In addition, certain activities can disqualify you from working in healthcare altogether—for example, committing a hate crime or act of terrorism. So if you like, post, or share any jokes or memes related to these subjects, you may never have an opportunity to work in healthcare—even if you have a health degree.

JOB OFFERS AND SECURITY CLEARANCES

As mentioned, anything you post publicly can be viewed by anyone, including hiring managers. Some organizations have policies that prohibit employees from looking at the personal social media profiles of job candidates during the hiring process (with the exception of LinkedIn since it is a professional network). However, not all organizations have this type of policy, and anything found online about you can be used to evaluate your candidacy. Your digital footprint could prevent employers from hiring you if any activity is questionable or unethical or if it violates healthcare principles.

For most healthcare jobs, you will be required to undergo a background check. In addition, for some healthcare jobs, you will need a security clearance. Government agencies, the military, and companies that work on government or military contracts, for example, may require that you obtain a security clearance before they employ you. There are various levels of security clearance; *confidential*, *secret*, and *top secret* are the three common ones.

Security clearance investigations probe into many aspects of your life, including your social media activity. In 2016, James Clapper, the director of national intelligence, signed Security Executive Agent Directive 5, which "addresses the collection and use of publicly available social media information during conduct of personnel security background investigations and adjudications for determining initial or continued eligibility for access to classified national security information to hold a sensitive position and the retention of such information" (Office of the Director of National Intelligence 2016).

If publicly available social media information about you reveals any disqualifying information or contradicts the answers you provide to questions in interviews or on application forms, you may not be granted a security clearance. In one case, a judge denied an applicant's continued eligibility for security clearance because there was a discrepancy between his sworn testimony and his previous security clearance application (Tully 2016). Although the applicant said on his 2003 security clearance application that he used marijuana only occasionally, he admitted in 2014 during a follow-up investigation that "he used marijuana on a daily basis in college and thereafter twice per month."

As recommended earlier in this chapter, a best practice is to make your personal social media accounts private. In healthcare, our integrity and ethical principles are of utmost importance. You should scrutinize your profiles carefully and edit accordingly.

CAN YOU DELETE OR SCRUB YOUR ONLINE PRESENCE?

Data brokers (companies that aggregate data from public or private sources) are always evolving, and hackers continually seem to find new ways to breach online information, so it is unlikely that your information can or will ever disappear entirely from the internet. Therefore, monitoring your online presence and taking action to create a positive online persona and digital brand are all the more important.

Hackers, especially advanced and skilled ones, can retrieve a lot of information posted on the internet, even if it has been deleted. Thus, deleting something from a website doesn't necessarily mean it is permanently removed.

In some instances, you may need to minimize your online presence. There are ways you can secure your accounts and scrub your public information (see Honeywell 2018; Sumagaysay 2018). However, as emphasized here, there is no guarantee your information will be permanently removed from the internet.

Action Items

1. Make sure the privacy settings on all your social media accounts are set to private.
2. Clean up the content on the social networking sites you use.
3. Create separate social media accounts for professional or business use (if relevant).

CHAPTER SUMMARY

Social media can be fun and engaging, but the content you post or respond to can have devastating effects on your digital brand and career if you are not careful. Most online communication is written, not face-to-face. As a result, your digital footprint can easily be misinterpreted because your tone of voice and body language are not included in your messages. You must carefully consider how you word the content you post on the internet and how it may affect your online persona.

According to Dr. Albert Mehrabian, professor emeritus of psychology at the University of California, Los Angeles, face-to-face communication consists of three basic elements: words, tone of voice, and nonverbal behavior such as gestures and facial expressions. What's more, 93 percent of face-to-face communication is conveyed through tone of voice and nonverbal behavior, not words (International Organization for Judicial Training 2013).

RESOURCES

Facebook. "Basic Privacy Settings & Tools." www.facebook.com/help/325807937506242.

Instagram. "Privacy Settings and Information." https://help.instagram.com/196883487377501.

LinkedIn. "Understanding Your Privacy Settings." www.linkedin.com/help/linkedin/answer/92055/understanding-your-privacy-settings.

Twitter. "How to Protect Your Personal Information." https://help.twitter.com/en/safety-and-security/twitter-privacy-settings.

REFERENCES

Honeywell, L. 2018. "Staying Safe When You Say #MeToo." Published February 12. www.aclu.org/blog/privacy-technology/internet-privacy/staying-safe-when-you-say-metoo.

International Organization for Judicial Training. 2013. "Albert Mehrabian Communication Studies." Accessed September 13, 2019. www.iojt-dc2013.org/~/media/Microsites/Files/IOJT/11042013-Albert-Mehrabian-Communication-Studies.ashx.

Office of the Director of National Intelligence. 2016. "Security Executive Agent Directive 5: Collection, Use, and Retention of Publicly Available Social Media Information in Personnel Security Background Investigations and Adjudications." Published May 12. www.dni.gov/files/NCSC/documents/Regulations/SEAD_5.pdf.

Sumagaysay, L. 2018. "Can Anyone Ever Really Scrub Their Online Presence?" *Star Online*. Published September 25. www.thestar.com.my/tech/tech-news/2018/09/25/can-anyone-ever-really-scrub-their-online-presence.

Tully, M. B. 2016. "Can My Social Media Posts Hurt My Security Clearance?" *Military Times*. Published July 3. www.militarytimes.com/2016/07/03/can-my-social-media-posts-hurt-my-security-clearance/.

CHAPTER 12

Going Off-Screen

SOME ACTIVITIES DURING your job search are best done in person rather than digitally or online. Whether it's practicing professional behaviors or gaining experience in interpreting body language, this chapter examines the benefits of going off-screen and explores how doing so can enhance your job search activities.

CHAPTER KEYWORDS

- Off-screen
- Body language
- Visual cues
- Observational skills
- Networking

WHAT DOES "GOING OFF-SCREEN" MEAN?

Going off-screen means that you do things in person rather than digitally or online. At times during your job search, you will be required to go off-screen. For example, you may be asked to come in for a face-to-face (F2F) interview. Or perhaps your sister wants to introduce you to her new boss, whose cousin is a vice president of operations at your local hospital.

Going off-screen also gives you the opportunity to practice some soft skills that just might help you get a job. For example:

- Conversing professionally with others
- Displaying professional behaviors
- Understanding body language (both your own and that of others)
- Reading and interpreting visual and verbal cues

When you search for a job digitally, you are passive and impersonal in many respects. You access an application, complete it online, attach your resume, and click to submit. You can even use a digital document signature app. Going off-screen involves being more proactive—getting off the couch and actually doing something in person with other people. It's no longer about your convenience; you have to organize, plan, and practice time management skills because you are dealing with other people, many of whom have busy schedules.

EARLY CAREERIST CASE

Recognizing When It's Time to Go Off-Screen

You are currently searching for a job in the digital environment. You figure, "I've got this one." You are tech savvy and incredibly creative online. You have a well-developed social media network that includes online mentors, and you use professional chat rooms. You search for jobs everywhere, even while on the beach. You can perform online job searches any time you want because your laptop or smartphone is always within reach. For you, job searching is a matter of convenience:

- You submit resumes and job applications using digital web resources such as LinkedIn and Indeed.

- You reach out to your connections on social media to see what is happening with their job searches and to ask if anyone has heard about recent job postings.

- You check in with your online mentors.

- You do all of your job searching digitally.

- Then you sit back on your couch and wait for the job interviews and offers to come.

You wonder why everyone told you that searching for a job would be hard and time-consuming. So far, it has been a piece of cake. You find job postings online and submit resumes and applications. None of the applications you've submitted has resulted in a job just yet, but you have gotten acknowledgments that your applications have been received. So, you believe you are on track. And every day, you find more job postings online, especially on LinkedIn. You click and submit another application and resume. You can't imagine what all the fuss is about.

A friend of yours, Danny, recently had an interview using video conferencing software. However, since the interview, Danny has not heard from the employer. But Danny isn't worried—the interviewer told him they would be in touch. And like you, he keeps looking online and applying for additional positions.

Meanwhile, you're sitting on your couch thinking about your next step. You've spent three months searching for a job, and you have had no job offers or even an interview. Now what? Your online mentor suggests that it's time to go off-screen.

THE HIDDEN JOB MARKET

Even though the internet has made it easy to connect online, such digital connectivity may not be sufficient to get you a job. Sometimes, going offline may be more effective in your job search.

Did you know that most jobs aren't posted officially—that there is a "hidden" job market? The fact is, many jobs are filled internally or through referrals. Unless you have access to someone in the organization, or to someone else who knows about the job, you may not hear about such openings. Even if you know someone inside the organization, you may know them only through the internet. Meeting someone in person and having a F2F conversation allows you to engage with that person and connect on a more personal level (Honeycutt 2017). Such F2F interactions may eventually help you discover hidden jobs.

Applying for a job today has been made easier by the internet and online platforms such as LinkedIn, Indeed, and Monster, to name just a few. These platforms allow you to complete and submit your job applications online with the click of a mouse or trackpad. However, some career experts, including Steven Rothberg, founder of the job search website College Recruiter, believe that offline job searching may be a better and more effective way to find the job you want because the majority (80 percent) of jobs aren't publicly advertised (Hireo 2020). These jobs are part of the hidden job market. Thus, networking with people offline is critical. It leads to opportunities for F2F introductions, which in turn give you access to unlisted jobs and referrals (Belli 2017).

Any situation in which you meet new people is an opportunity for you to network at a deeper level than online. Even though there are no accurate statistics informing us how many jobs are available through offline interactions, you probably know or have heard about peers who have gotten tips about job openings at networking events. Because timing is important in a job search, you may wonder how much luck is involved in running into someone—just the right person—who can help you. But it's not about finding someone to help you—it's about you finding a job.

Networking may be a gateway to landing an interview before other applicants (and perhaps ultimately landing a job offer). However, professional networking events require you to be proactive. A lot of preparation and planning are involved, and your competition also will be attending these events.

PROFESSIONAL EVENTS AS NETWORKING OPPORTUNITIES

You may have first heard about professional conferences and meetings when you were in school or early in your career. Some of these events may even take place in your local community. For example, the American College of Healthcare Executives has local and state chapters, most of which schedule regular meetings with guest speakers from nearby healthcare organizations, consulting firms, and government agencies.

Attending professional meetings in person is an excellent way for you to hone professional behaviors and practice your conversation skills. Talking with classmates in school is very different from conversing with others in a professional setting. You need to use the vocabulary, terminology, and even jargon of your profession and be conversant in current topics and industry trends. You need to address people in a professional manner, as opposed to how you might do so in casual conversation.

You also need to dress professionally. At the professional meetings you attend, take time to observe how attendees are dressed. How does a vice president of a large health system dress compared with a consultant or a professor? How are you dressed compared with your peers (who are also your competition)?

You may notice that some attendees are dressed in business attire even though the invitation indicated that business casual was acceptable. They are likely coming from work. This gives you a chance to observe how they dress in their workplace setting. Did you dress in business attire when you had your recent video interview? No? Next time, try it.

Action Items

1. Decide whether you're dressing for the job you want.
2. Go through your closet and separate your business clothes from your business casual clothes.

UNDERSTANDING WHAT THE MEETING IS REALLY ABOUT

Attending a professional meeting or conference can be a learning experience if you observe others. Observing people is a skill—a soft skill. Your observations will provide you with information about how to behave, especially when moving around the room.

Recall that at your last professional event, you were introduced to several people to whom you had sent your resume but then never received an acknowledgment. You immediately asked them why you didn't get a response from them. They looked perplexed and went silent. As soon as they had the opportunity, they moved away from you. What did you miss? What should you have been paying attention to? You realize the following:

- This is a professional meeting, not the office or human resources (HR) department. It is not the place to ask people why you didn't get an interview or response to your application, especially if they don't work in HR.
- This is the place for you to make contacts with those inside an organization you're interested in. Knowing an insider can be helpful in your job search. For example, you may be

able to ask that person what type of skills are preferred or if you need any specific certification or training to get hired.

- This is the place for you to further develop contacts made at earlier meetings and events—for example, over coffee or lunch. At the same time, you can observe the behaviors and skills of these people, and see how yours compare.
- These people are extremely well spoken. They illustrate their points by referencing books they recently read or podcasts they have listened to.
- These people also have very professional manners.

Important Tips

- Don't behave like a stalker.
- Don't approach everyone as a job contact. They aren't.
- Start out with casual conversation. Be sure to listen to introductions.
- Don't monopolize the conversation.
- If someone asks if you have a business card, hand it over. Same with a resume.
- Learn to read visual cues and body language. If people aren't interested in you, move on.
- Always demonstrate professionalism. Be polite and stay positive.

TRAINING, JOB FAIRS, AND VOLUNTEERING

In addition to professionally sponsored events, training programs, job fairs, and volunteer activities afford you opportunities to practice being a professional and to learn more about healthcare than through what you read or see online.

A number of training programs are offered in both online and F2F formats. Even though online training may appeal to you because of its convenience, try F2F too, which enables you to meet new people. You can have coffee with them before or after the training session.

At job fairs, you can meet prospective employers (usually HR representatives) in person. HR representatives can be a fountain of information about organizations you're interested in, so ask questions. You can also see how much competition you have (by looking at the number of attendees) and how you present compared with your competitors. Consider the following questions:

- Are you courteous, polite, and enthusiastic?
- Are you able to ask substantive questions related to the employing organization?
- Do you have a hard copy of your resume to hand out?

Volunteering in healthcare is another way you can practice your professional communication skills and interpretation of body language. It is also an opportunity to learn more about the field. Whether you volunteer in a hospital, local public health department, or nonprofit charity, you are gaining a more complete picture of your field. You are likely interacting with patients, too. Remember:

- During any F2F encounter, be sure you have a hard copy of your resume to hand to anyone you speak with who appears interested in you. They can review it and ask you questions on-site.
- You can add a digital component to your business card— for example, a quick-response (QR) code that links to your online resume. A type of matrix barcode, QR codes have gained widespread use. For example, instead of presenting a paper boarding pass, you can download a QR code on your smartphone and show it at the gate.

Tips for Spending Time Off-Screen

- Tell everyone you are searching for a job—not just those in your professional network but also people you encounter regularly. You might be surprised who knows of a job opening—it could be a neighbor or someone on the elevator.

- Drop off your resume or job application in person—it just might give you an advantage.

- Always behave professionally in the F2F world. You never know whom you might encounter, or where. Healthcare CEOs are human, too, and you just might find yourself waiting in line with them at the DMV (department of motor vehicles).

BODY LANGUAGE

Why is body language important? Because people form 90 percent of their opinion of you within the first four minutes, even if they haven't met or spoken with you (Pease and Pease 2004).

Body language is a two-way street. The body language you demonstrate conveys messages to other people, including how you are receiving their messages. Conversely, you need to be able to read and interpret the body language of others, from posture and gestures to facial expressions and eye movements.

Watch what happens when you are speaking with someone: They either nod in agreement while you speak, or they shake their head slightly from side to side. Which person is agreeing with you? This is an easy one—it's the head nodder.

But suppose you're being interviewed and you notice that the interviewer touches her chin and then crosses her arms. What is she signaling to you? This example is more complicated than the preceding one because most people tend to touch their chins when they are making a decision. If the interviewer's subsequent movement includes open arms, she has likely viewed you positively. Crossed arms, however, mean the opposite: She won't be offering you a job (Pease and Pease 2004).

Tips for Face-to-Face Encounters

- If a hand is extended, shake hands. Using the right hand is customary. The handshake should be brief and firm (though not a death grip) and limited to one hand.

- Always display a positive, upbeat manner and smile naturally.

- Demonstrate openness by keeping both palms and arms open.

- Never create a barrier by folding your arms or holding your arms in front of you.

- Laugh if it feels natural and appropriate to what is being said.

- Display an animated face to show enthusiasm.

- Use expressive gestures, but don't overdo them.

- Always keep your chin up so as not to create a negative environment.

- Stand straight when speaking, and lean forward when listening.

- Stand as close as you feel comfortable. If the other person moves back, don't move forward—they are signaling that you were too close. Staying in place indicates "message received."

Source: Pease and Pease (2004).

> **Action Item**
>
> 1. Watch the following video on body language (more precisely, the use of hands and handshaking):
>   - "Body Language: The Power Is in the Palm of Your Hands" (see Pease 2013 in References section)

CHAPTER SUMMARY

Healthcare organizations are human services organizations. When you work in healthcare, you likely will have a great deal of interaction with patients and other humans, especially if you are an early careerist in an entry-level position. F2F communication is simply a big part of the industry.

Going off-screen is important at times, especially as you advance in your career. F2F interviews become increasingly likely as you climb the professional ladder, assume more responsibility, and earn more income. Prospective healthcare employers will want to see firsthand that you behave professionally and can communicate knowledgably and enthusiastically.

Ways you can spend your time off-screen include, but are not limited to, the following:

1. Make connections with people through F2F professional networking.

2. Develop relationships with members of your professional network. Suggest attending another meeting together, or invite them for coffee. If they decline, try again later. If you receive a second rejection, let it go.

3. Meet regularly F2F with members of your professional network. Create a schedule and make sure you do something once a week.

4. Always be ready for a potential interview. Use F2F occasions to develop your soft skills and your ability to converse and behave professionally.

EARLY CAREERIST CASE

Setting Realistic Goals

Malik recently graduated with a master's degree in health policy and management. Following the advice of some of his peers, he was attending his first professional healthcare networking event. His goal for the evening was to meet at least two professionals who were working in organizations in which he might like to find employment. He planned to exchange contact information and, if they were interested, to send them his resume.

Malik's peers had advised him to be enthusiastic and, above all, to be sure to listen to everyone he spoke with. Malik followed their advice and managed to meet three professionals, all of whom were interested in him, and one of whom invited him to make an appointment for an office tour and possibly lunch later in the week.

As Malik departed the event, he ran into a former classmate, Leah, who described the event as a waste of time. Leah's goals for the event were to meet as many people as possible and to exchange contact information with everyone she met. Leah was optimistic as she made her way to the exit until she found some of her business cards discarded on tables and even dropped on the floor. When Malik suggested that she should perhaps have used a targeted approach and met fewer people, Leah shrugged and said, "Not my style. Waste of time to meet only two or three people."

Three months later, Malik had landed a job as a result of the contact he had made at the networking social. Malik had followed up, met the contact for lunch, and gotten a tour of the offices at the organization he was interested in.

A few weeks after he started, Malik attended another professional networking event and ran into Leah. Leah was shocked that Malik had found a job through the contact he had made at the previous event. "You got lucky," she told him, and instead of asking Malik for more details about his new job, she sped off to meet as many attendees as possible. Malik didn't get a chance to tell Leah that his new employer was hiring, and three positions had just been posted.

RESOURCE

Franklin, L. 2017. "Reading Minds Through Body Language." www.youtube.com/watch?v=W3P3rT0j2gQ.

REFERENCES

Belli, G. 2017. "How Many Jobs Are Found Through Networking, Really?" PayScale. Published April 6. www.payscale.com/career-news/2017/04/many-jobs-found-networking.

Hireo. 2020. "8 Steps to Start Job Search Offline." Accessed February 5. www.hireoapp.com/posts/17-8-steps-to-start-job-search-offline.

Honeycutt, L. 2017. "The Importance of Face-to-Face Networking in a Digital World." Entrepreneur. Published February 6. www.entrepreneur.com/article/288530.

Pease, A. 2013. "Body Language: The Power Is in the Palm of Your Hands." YouTube. Published November 17. www.youtube.com/watch?v=ZZZ7k8cMA-4.

Pease, A., and B. Pease. 2004. *The Definitive Book of Body Language: The Hidden Meaning Behind People's Gestures and Expressions.* New York: Bantam Books.

Index

Note: Italicized page locators refer to exhibits.

Abilities: understanding, 7, 13
ACHE. *See* American College of
    Healthcare Executives
Adler, Lou, viii, 109
Advanced degrees: factors to consider
    relative to, 69–70
Agency for Healthcare Research and
    Quality, 65
AI. *See* Artificial intelligence
Alumni mixers, 112
Amazon, 66
American College of Healthcare
    Executives (ACHE), 78; annual
    Congress on Healthcare Leadership,
    112; CareerEDGE, 10; Healthcare
    Executive Competencies Assessment
    Tool, 10; Interview Prep Tool, 100,
    104; Job Center, 53, 61; local and state
    chapter meetings, 135
American Diabetes Association, 65
American Heart Association, 65
American Hospital Association, 65
American Public Health Association
    annual conference: university
    alumni mixer at, 112
Appearance: dressing for the job you
    want, 33, 95–96, 117, 135–36
Apple devices: FaceTime for, 93, 104, 117
Applicant tracking systems (ATSs), 76,
    77–78, 79, 82, 83, 84, 87
Articles, online, 65
Artificial intelligence (AI), 87; growing
    use of, 76; interviewing with, 91
Artificial intelligence interviews: what to
    watch for and do during, 101–2

Association of Schools and Program of
    Public Health, 53
ATSs. *See* Applicant tracking systems
Attire: professional, 33, 135–36
Audio books, 66
Authority: building around your digital
    brand, 37
Avatar: classroom, 33

Background checks, 125–26
Barnard, Frederick, 121
Becker's Hospital Review, 69
Bing, 2
Blogs, 40, 65, 72
Body language, 138, 139–41; action
    items, 141; artificial intelligence
    interviews and, 102; importance of,
    139; understanding, 132
Bots: being interviewed by, 91, 101, 103;
    resume screening by, 77
Buffett, Warren, 63
Bureau of Labor Statistics: on average
    amount of years spent at a job, 31
Business attire, 135–36
Business cards, 137; QR codes added
    to, 138
Business social media accounts:
    personal accounts separated from,
    123, 127

Career advancement: professional online
    presence essential to, viii
Career Anchors self-assessment, 10
Career Builder: Harris Poll for, 31;
    thank-you notes survey, 102

CareerBuilder.com, 61
Career choices: reasons behind, 52
CareerEDGE (American College of
    Healthcare Executives), 10
Career goals, 7–8. *See also* Self-determined
    career
Career opportunities: venturing beyond
    healthcare field, 28
Career plans: establishing, 51. *See also*
    Three-year career plans
Centers for Medicare & Medicaid
    Services, 65
Certifications: earning relevant, 67–68;
    examples of, for healthcare
    positions, 58; job postings and, 56;
    three-year career plan and, 57–58
Certified Professional in Healthcare
    Quality (CPHQ), 68
Certified Professional in Healthcare Risk
    Management (CPHRM), 68
Certified Professional in Patient Safety
    (CPPS), 68
Chatbots: being interviewed by, 91, 101
Clapper, James, 126
Classroom avatar: headshot selected
    for, 33
Clinical licenses, 56
Clinical Social Work Association, 65
Clothing: professional, 95–96, 117,
    135–36
Co-branding, 41–42
CollegeRecruiter, 134
Competition: job fairs and, 138
Conferences, 111–13, 135–36; meeting
    people at, 111; meeting presenters
    at, 112; presenting at, 112; social
    mixers at, 112; tips for, 136–37
Confidential security clearance level, 126
Consistency: in digital brand, 41, 43
Continuing education, 58, 67
Conversation skills, 135, 137
Cover letters: avoiding common mistakes
    in, 81; screening, 76; writing, 80–82
CPHQ. *See* Certified Professional in
    Healthcare Quality
CPHRM. *See* Certified Professional in
    Healthcare Risk Management
CPPS. *See* Certified Professional in
    Patient Safety

Credibility: expertise and, 35
Curricula vitae (CVs): resumes vs., 76–77
Cybersecurity threats, 53

Data brokers, 126
Data-related healthcare jobs: rise in,
    52–53
Deception, 22
Deleting online presence: issues related
    to, 126–27
Deloitte's Global Millennial Study, 31
Digital age: living in, 1
Digital authenticity, 17, 28
Digital brand: checklist, 48; consistency
    of, 41; monitoring and evaluating,
    41–42; positive, creating, 127; start
    of, 33
Digital brand equity, 41
Digital brand identity: creating, 41
Digital branding components, checklist
    of, 40–42; co-branding, 41–42;
    digital brand equity, 41; digital
    brand identity, 41; digital brand
    integration, 41
Digital brand integration, 41
Digital brand recovery, 45–46
Digital document signature app, 132
Digital footprint: job candidacy and
    impact of, 1, 125
Digital magazines, 66–67, 73
Digital mentors, 18, 23–25, 28
Digital networking, 107–14, 117; action
    items, 113; conferences, 111–13;
    e-mail, 110; LinkedIn, 109–10;
    resources, 114; social media,
    110–11
Digital persona: self-creation of, 18–19
Digital profile, 6; authentic, 17; routine
    scanning of, 28
Digital rebranding: definition of, 45
Digital self-branding, 31–48, 116; action
    items, 35; basic components for,
    40–42; branding yourself as a
    product, 34–35; checklist, 48; as
    continuous process, 47; distinguish-
    ing your offline and online brands,
    32–33; establishing, developing,
    and displaying expertise on social
    media, 35–38, *36*; extending brand

image through influencers, 46–47; identifying your unique selling points, 38–40; importance of, 47; monitoring and evaluating your digital brand, 43–44, 48; overlooking what makes you stand out, 42–43; performance assessment metrics for, 44, *45*; social media handle and, 34

Digital self-evaluation assessment tool, 19, *20–21*

Digital self-perception, 17–29, 116; action items, 19, 23; definition of, 17; importance of, 18; realistic, 19, 22–23; understanding role of, 17

DISC assessment tool, 10

Disney World: customer experience principles at, 64

Distractions: eliminating, for online interviews, 94–95

Diversity: online communication in light of, 123, 125

Dressing for the job you want, 33, 95–96, 117, 135–36

Due diligence, 18, 26

Early Careerist Cases: contacting the organization without permission, 85–86; overlooking what makes you stand out, 42–43; reaching out for online mentors, 24–25; recognizing when it's time to go off-screen, 132–33; setting realistic goals, 142–43

E-books, 66–67, 73

Education requirement: job postings and, 56

E-mail, viii, 109, 110, 117

Emotional intelligence: assessments, 11; definition and components of, 9

Empathy, 9

Employers: applicant tracking systems used by, 76, 77–78, 79; level of scrutiny by, 32; online presence and hiring by, vii; online resources at disposal of, 23; real you and, 18; researching, 26–27

Environmental distractions: eliminating, for online interviews, 94–95

E-signatures, 83

Evaluation: definition of, 115. *See also* Self–evaluation

Expertise: definition of, 35; developing, social media and, 37; examples of, *36*; sufficient demonstrated, 36

Extended DISC Individual Assessment, 10

Eye contact: artificial intelligence interviews and, 102; during interviews, 100

Facebook, 1, 27, 37, 38, 40, 46, 108, 109, 113, 121, 123, 124; accounts, analyzing, 19; digital brand integration and, 41; percentage of users in United States, 111; on tagging, 5

FaceTime, 93, 104, 117

Face-to-face (F2F) interactions: basic elements in communication, 128; at conferences, 111–13; hidden job market and, 134; interviews, 91, 96, 132, 141; networking, viii, 109; offline brand and, 33; tips for, 140; training programs, 138

FACHE. *See* Fellow of the American College of Healthcare Executives

Facial expressions, 102, 128, 139

Fellow of the American College of Healthcare Executives (FACHE), 58

Filters, 77

Firefox, 2

FIRO-B. *See* Fundamental Interpersonal Relations Orientation-Behavior (FIRO-B)

Following up: after interviews, 102–3; on job applications, 83–84

Fonts: for cover letter, 81; for resume, 79

Formatting: of resume, 79

Fundamental Interpersonal Relations Orientation-Behavior (FIRO-B), 9

Gates, Bill, 63

GEIT. *See* Global Emotional Intelligence Test

Gestures, 128, 139, 140

Glassdoor, 27, 29, 61, 97, 98

Global EI Capability Assessment (Global Leadership Foundation), 11

Global Emotional Intelligence Test (GEIT), 11
Goals: career, 7–8; long-term, 7; mapping, to your three-year plan, 59, *60*; realistic, setting, 142–43; realistic vs. unrealistic, 8; short-term, 7; SMART, 8
Going off-screen, 131–43; body language, 139–41; hidden job market, 134–35; meaning of phrase, 131–32; practicing soft skills and, 132; professional events, 135–36; recognizing when it is time for, 132–33; tips for, 139; training, job fairs, and volunteering, 137–38; understanding what professional meeting is really about, 136–37
Google, 2, 27, 61
Google Chat, 93
Google Chrome, 2
Google Hangouts, 93, 99, 104, 117
Google Sheets, 83
Googling yourself, 1–2, 116; action items, 6; after making improvements to online persona, 118; checking image results, 5; sample searches, *4*; searching by name and keywords, 3–5, *4*, 6

Hackers, 126, 127
Hair: online interviews and, 96, 100
Handshakes, 140
Hands-on practice, 67, 73
Hangouts Chat, 93
Hangouts Meet, 93
Hard job skills, 56
Harris Poll: for Career Builder, 31
Headhunters, 87, 88
Headphones, 95
Headsets: testing, 93
Headshots: professional, 33
Healthcare Executive, 69
Healthcare Executive Competencies Assessment Tool (American College of Healthcare Executives), 10
Healthcare industry: retail industry's influence on, 101
Healthcare organizations: contacting, without permission, 85–86; as human services organizations, 141; interacting with, via social media, 110–11
Healthcare trends: keeping up with, 69
Health eCareers, 62
Hidden job market, 134–35
HIPAA (Health Insurance Portability and Accountability Act) audits, 22
Hiring: costs, 101; digital footprint and, 125; online presence and decisions related to, 31–32
Honesty, 18
Hospital Careers, 62
Hospital Jobs, 62
Hospital Jobs Online, 62
"How to Get Your Resume Past Resume Screening Software" (video), 80
"How to Prepare for an Online Skype Job Interview," 100
"How to Prepare for Video Interviews," 100
Humanoids: being interviewed by, 101
Human resources: artificial intelligence screens and, 76; meeting representatives at job fairs, 138

IBM, 76
Identity theft: preventing, 5
Image results: checking, 5. *See also* Photos and pictures
Improvement: continuous cycle of, 119
Indeed.com, viii, 27, 29, 53, 61, 97, 133, 134
Influencers: action items, 47; definition of, 46; extending brand image through, 46–47; in healthcare, identifying, 47
Information technology healthcare jobs: rise in, 53
Instagram, 1, 38, 40, 46, 113, 121, 124; accounts, analyzing, 19; digital brand integration and, 41; percentage of users in United States, 111
Instant messaging, 109
Intangible factors: examples of, 34
Intent: living with, 108
Internet, 1, 121, 127, 134. *See also* Social media

Internet Explorer, 2
Internships, 24
Interviews, 91–104, 117; action items,
100; advance planning and preparation for, 92–95; artificial intelligence,
what to watch for and do during,
101–2; dress for the job you want,
95–96; eliminating environmental
distractions, 94–95; face-to-face
(F2F), 91, 96, 132, 141; making
sure technology works, 92–93; in
online environment, 33; potential,
being ready for, 142; practicing for,
99–100; primary goal of, 98;
questions commonly asked in,
97–98; resources, 104; smartphone,
95; success with, tips for, 98–99;
thank-you notes after, 102–3
*In Their Time: The Greatest Business
Leaders of the 20th Century* (Mayo &
Nohria), 12

Job applications: collecting, via social
media, vii; online, 82–83; screening,
76; tracking, 83
Job boards: general, 61; healthcare,
61–62; online, search terms for, 53;
search terms and, examples of, *54*
Job descriptions: action items, 57; job
skills listed in, 59; regular review of,
52–53; what to look for in, 54–57
Job fairs, 137, 138
Job offers: security clearances and, 125–26
Job opportunities: LinkedIn All-Star
status and, 110
Job positions: certifications and, 68;
three-year career plan and, 59
Job postings: action items, 57; getting
past resume screens, 78; matching
qualifications with those listed in, 81;
regular review of, 52–53, 59; reviewing, 119; what to look for in, 54–57
Job preparation, 75–89, 117; in the digital
age, 76, 117; following up, 83–84;
online job applications, 82–83;
resources, 88–89; resume vs. curriculum vitae and, 76–77; using outside
resources, 86–87; writing a cover letter, 80–82; writing a resume, 77–80

Jobs: requirements/qualifications for,
55–56; responsibilities in, 55; titles
of, 22, 54
Job search process: challenges related to,
86, 88. *See also* Going off-screen
Job skills, 55; hard and soft, 56; new,
prioritizing learning about, 64;
three-year career plan and, 59
Jobs2Careers, 61
Joint Commission, 65
Journals: online, 71–72
Jung, Carl, 11
Jung Typology Test, 11

Keywords: for getting past resume
screens, 78; searching yourself by
name and, 3–5, *4, 6*
Knowledge, skills, and abilities (KSAs),
18, 19

Leadership: assessments of, 12; tracking
examples of, 25, 26
Leadership perception: in online
environment, 25, *26*
Lean, 68
Learning assessments, 12
Licenses: examples of, for healthcare
positions, 58; listed in job
postings, 56; three-year career
plan and, 57–58
Life-long learning: success and, 63, 71,
117, 119
Lighting: for digital interviews, 94
LinkedIn, viii, 4, 27, 37, 38, 40, 46, 61, 79,
80, 81, 82, 97, 117, 123, 124, 125, 133,
134; connecting with conference
presenters via, 112; digital brand
integration and, 41; examining your
profile, 19; mobile app, 110; networking and, 109–10; online mentors,
connecting with, 23–24; profile
levels in, 109; profiles of prospective
employers, 27; reaching All-Star status
on, 109, 110; tailoring your networking efforts with, 112–13
Location field: job postings and, 53
Long-term goals, 7
Lying: avoiding during interviews, 98; on
resumes, 22

Magazines: digital, 66–67, 73
Manners: professional, 137
Marketing: digital branding as form of, 34
Mayo, Anthony J., 12
MBTI. *See* Myers-Briggs Type Indicator
Mehrabian, Albert, 128
Memes, 125
Mentoring relationships: LinkedIn,
23–24. *See also* Online mentors
Metrics: for brand performance and
associated outcomes, 44, *45*
Microphones: testing, 93
Microsoft Edge, 2
Millennials: job tenures and, 31
MindTools' "How Emotionally Intelligent
Are You?," 11
Modern Healthcare, 69
Monster.com, 28, 29, 61, 78, 134
Motivation, 9
Musk, Elon, 63, 68
Myers, Isabel Briggs, 11
Myers-Briggs Type Indicator (MBTI), 9
My Interview Simulator—Online Edition,
100, 104

National Committee for Quality
Assurance, 53
Networking: going off-screen tips for,
139; hidden job market and, 134–35;
with intent, 108, 113, 117; with
many people, 108; other face-to-face
events, 113; professional online
presence essential to, viii; purpose
of, 107. *See also* Digital networking
New Enneagram Test, 11
Nohria, Nitin, 12
Nonverbal behaviors, 128
Nurse.com jobs, 62
Nursing jobs, 62

Objectives: mapping to your three-year
plan, 59, *60*
Observing people, 136
Offline brand: online brand distinguished
from, 32–33
Omissions on resume: employer detec-
tion of, 46
"One Look Is Worth a Thousand Words"
(Barnard), 121

Online and digital resources for learning
new skills, 65–67, 71–73; e-books
and digital magazines, 66–67;
hands-on practice, 67; online
articles and blogs, 65; online training, 66; online videos, 65; podcasts,
66; university alumni resources, 67
Online brand: offline brand distinguished
from, 32–33
Online interviews: advantages with,
91, 103
Online job applications, 82–83
Online journals, 71–72
Online mentors, 133; accessing, 23;
monitoring/evaluating perceptions
of, 29; reaching out for, 24–25
Online peers: digital self-perception and,
23–24, 27; monitoring/evaluating
perceptions of, 29
Online persona: accurate appraisal of,
18; cleaning up, 2, 32
Online presence: hiring decisions and,
31–32; monitoring, 127
Online training, 66, 71, 72
Online videos, 65, 71
Open-access assessment tools, 11–12,
14–15; emotional intelligence
assessments, 11; leadership assessments, 12; learning assessments,
12; personality assessments, 11
Organizational culture: determining
personal fit with, 25–27, 28
Outside resources: using, 86–87

PayScale, 27, 29
Performance assessment metrics: digital
brand, 44, *45*
Personality assessments, 11
Personality type theory, 11
Personal social media accounts: business
accounts separated from, 123, 127;
making private, 122, 127
Photo album: professional, 35
Photos and pictures: inappropriate,
removing, 123; privacy settings and,
122; professional headshots, 33;
tagging, 5; viral, 121
Pinterest, 124
Planning: for interviews, 91, 92–95

Podcasts, 66, 71, 72
Polarized topics: avoiding, on social media, 124
Posts on social media: cleaning up, 123–24; strategic communication and, 124–25
Posture, 139, 140; artificial intelligence interviews and, 102; online interviews and, 100
Preferred qualifications, 55
Presenters: at conferences, 112
Previous experience: job postings and, 56
Price Group's "True Leader" quiz, 12
Privacy, 121; personal social media accounts and, 122; settings, 122, 127
Probation, 22
Professional certifications, 56
Professional events: as networking opportunities, 135–36
Professional goal achievements: identifying, 41, 48
Professional image photo: revisiting, 35
Professionalism: demonstrated, 137
Professional meetings: tips for, 136–37
Professional network: building, 107, 117; meeting regularly with, 14
Professional photo album: creating, 35
Profiles: cleaning up content on, 123–24; LinkedIn and levels of, 109–10; school, 33
Public Health Employment Connection, 62
Public Health Jobs, 53, 62
Public information: scrubbing, 127
Punctuality: digital interviews and, 99

Quick-response (QR) codes: adding, to business cards, 138

Reading: self-learning through, 68–69
Realistic goal setting, 142–43
Rebranding: definition of, 45
Recruiters, 86–87, 88, 102
Referrals, 134
Reputational enhancement: co-branding and, 42
Required qualifications, 55
Respect: online communication and, 124

Resumes, 117, 133, 137, 138, 139; curricula vitae vs., 76–77; evaluating, 119; formatting for, 79; lying on, 22; online job applications and, 82; reviewing, 19; screening, 76; updating, 32; writing, 77–78
Resume screening software: increased use of, 77
Resume screens: getting past, 78–80
Retail industry: influence on healthcare, 101
Robots, 77, 78, 82, 91
Rometty, Ginni, 76
Rothberg, Steven, 134

Safari, 2
Saint-Exupéry, Antoine de, 61
Salary: data on, 27; expectations, interview questions about, 98; job responsibilities and, 55
Sapp, J., 8
Schein, Edgar, 10
School profile: headshot selected for, 33
Scientific journals, 65
Screenshots, 123, 125
Scrubbing online presence: issues related to, 126–27
Search engines: accessing, 2
Searching yourself by name and keyword, 3–5, 4, 6
Search terms: for online job boards, 53, 54
Secret security clearance level, 126
Security clearance investigations, 126
Security clearances: job offers and, 125–26; levels of, 126
Security Executive Agent Directive 5, 126
Self-assessment: improvement and, 119; tools, 9–10, 14
Self-awareness, 9
Self-determination: definition of, 52
Self-determined career, 51–62, 116; action items, 60; creating a three-year career plan, 57–59; definition of, 52; mapping goals/objectives to your three-year plan, 59, 60; regularly review job postings and descriptions, 52–53; resources, 61–62; what to look for in job postings and job descriptions, 54–57

Self-discovery, 7–15, 116; action items, 13; career goals, 7–8; various meanings of term, 7

Self-evaluation, 115–20; action items, 120; description of, 118; improvement and, 119; ongoing process of, 115, 120; reviewing what you have learned about, 115–17

Self-learning, 63–74, 117, 119; earning relevant certifications, 67–68; job skills and, 56; online and digital resources for, 65–67, 71–73; prioritizing learning new job skills, 64; reading and, 68–69; returning to school, what to consider, 69–70

Self-regulation, 9

Selling points: unique, identifying, 38–40

Short-term goals, 7

SimplyHired, 61

Six degrees of separation theory, 108

Six Sigma, 68

Skill building: prioritizing, 64

Skills: falsifying, 22

Skype, 33, 93, 104, 117

SMART goals, 8

Smartphone: interviews, suggestions for, 95; submitting job applications on, 83

Snapchat, 27, 124

Social media, viii, 1, 23, 109, 113, 121–28, 133; accounts, monitoring and updating, 28; action items, 127; cleaning up content on, 123–24; controversial content on, 121; deleting or scrubbing online presence, 126–27; establishing, developing, and displaying expertise on, 35–38, 36; job applications screened via, vii; job offers, security clearances, and, 125–26; "liking" and "unliking" on, 123, 125; making personal accounts private, 122–23, 127; networking with, 110–11; resources, 128. See also Facebook; Instagram; LinkedIn; Twitter

Social media groups: finding and joining, 37

Social media handle: definition of, 34

Social mixers: at conferences, 112

Social proof: definition of, 36; examples of, 36; for your unique selling points, 40

Social skills, 9

Soft job skills, 56

SpaceX, 63

Strengths: understanding, 7, 13, 59

Tagging photos, 5

Tangible factors: examples of, 34

Technical certifications, 56

Technology: online interviews mediated by, 91, 92–93

TED Talks, 65, 71

Texts, 109

Thank-you notes: sending, after interviews, 102–3

Three-year career plans, 119; certifications and licenses, 57–58; considering different aspects of, 57; creating, 57–59; job positions, 59; job skills, 59; mapping goals and objectives to, 59; sample career plan and map, 60

Timeline for goals and objectives: creating, 60, 60

Time management skills: going off-line and, 132

Tone of voice, 128

Top-secret security clearance level, 126

Training: online, 66, 71, 72; programs, 137

"True Leader" quiz (Price Group), 12

Tuition programs, 69

Twitter, 1, 27, 38, 40, 111, 113, 124; accounts, analyzing, 19; digital brand integration and, 41

Unethical employers: digital rebranding and, 45–46

Unique selling points (USPs): action items, 39; identifying, 38–40; supporting, evidence or social proof for, 40

University alumni resources, 67

USAJOBS, 61, 77

USPs. See Unique selling points

VARK questionnaire, 12

Verbal cues: reading and interpreting, 132

Video conferences, 109
Video conferencing software, 93
Videos: online, 65, 71; viral, 121
Vimeo, 65
Visual cues: in artificial intelligence
    interviews, 102; reading and
    interpreting, 132
Volunteering, 37, 119, 137, 138

Weaknesses: understanding, 7, 13, 59
Web browsers, 2
Webcam: online job interviews
    conducted via, 92

Webinars, 109
"Which Type of Leader Are You?"
    (Mayo), 12
White, Amy, 23
Winfrey, Oprah, 63
Work values test, 12
Writing: cover letter, 80–82; resume,
    77–78

Yahoo!, 2
YouTube, 65, 124, 125

ZipRecruiter, 61

About the Authors

Donna Malvey, PhD, is an associate professor in the Department of Health Management and Informatics at the University of Central Florida. She received her MHSA degree from the George Washington University and completed an administrative residency and postgraduate fellowship in health systems at the VA Medical Center in Washington, DC. She earned her PhD in Administration-Health Services at the University of Alabama at Birmingham and received a national award from Sodexho Marriott for her dissertation research on medical group practices. Dr. Malvey also served as an adjunct associate professor of healthcare leadership at Brown University, where she taught in the Executive Healthcare Management and Leadership program.

Dr. Malvey has published extensively in the healthcare field, including several articles in the *Journal of Healthcare Management.* Most recently, she has published her original research in book format. She is coauthor of *mHealth: Transforming Healthcare* (Springer, 2014) and *The Retail Revolution in Health Care* (Praeger, 2010). She is also a coeditor and contributing author of *The Handbook of Healthcare Management* (Elgar, 2015).

Jessica Sapp, DrPH, is an associate professor in the School of Health Sciences at American Public University System. She has more than 15 years of experience in public health, working in government, hospital, health insurance, community, international, corporate, and academic settings. She earned her DrPH in Health Policy and Management at Georgia Southern University; her MPH in Health Promotion, Education and Behavior at the University of South Carolina; and her BS in Health Science Education at the University of Florida.

Dr. Sapp has held various leadership positions in healthcare and has developed early careerists. She has implemented internship programs, served as a preceptor, and was the internship director for the Health Services Administration program at the University of Central Florida. Dr. Sapp has prepared students for internships and, guided by her experience hiring healthcare employees, has assisted them in searching and applying for jobs, developing their resumes, preparing for interviews, and building their skills. Dr. Sapp is well versed in creating digital profiles and online branding.